The joy of t
Golf Ball, L
Refrigerato
succession, lies in encountering the various
turns through which each of their authors has
been put by his or her object. . . . The object
predominates, sits squarely center stage, directs
the action. The object decides the genre,
the chronology, and the limits of the study.
Accordingly, the author has to take her cue
from the *thing* she chose or that chose her. The
result is a wonderfully uneven series of books,
each one a *thing* unto itself."

Julian Yates, *Los Angeles Review of Books*

The Object Lessons series has a beautifully
simple premise. Each book or essay centers
on a specific object. This can be mundane or
unexpected, humorous or politically timely.
Whatever the subject, these descriptions reveal
the rich worlds hidden under the surface of
things."

Christine Ro, *Book Riot*

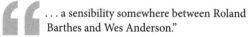

. . . a sensibility somewhere between Roland
Barthes and Wes Anderson."

Simon Reynolds, author of *Retromania:*
Pop Culture's Addiction to Its Own Past

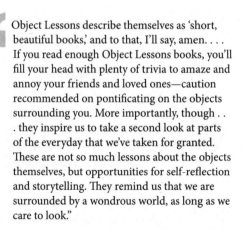

The Object Lessons series achieves something very close to magic: the books take ordinary— even banal—objects and animate them with a rich history of invention, political struggle, science, and popular mythology. Filled with fascinating details and conveyed in sharp, accessible prose, the books make the everyday world come to life. Be warned: once you've read a few of these, you'll start walking around your house, picking up random objects, and musing aloud: 'I wonder what the story is behind this thing?'"

Steven Johnson, author of *Where Good Ideas Come From* and *How We Got to Now*

Object Lessons describe themselves as 'short, beautiful books,' and to that, I'll say, amen. . . . If you read enough Object Lessons books, you'll fill your head with plenty of trivia to amaze and annoy your friends and loved ones—caution recommended on pontificating on the objects surrounding you. More importantly, though . . . they inspire us to take a second look at parts of the everyday that we've taken for granted. These are not so much lessons about the objects themselves, but opportunities for self-reflection and storytelling. They remind us that we are surrounded by a wondrous world, as long as we care to look."

John Warner, *The Chicago Tribune*

OBJECTLESSONS

A book series about the hidden lives of ordinary things.

Series Editors:

Ian Bogost and Christopher Schaberg

Advisory Board:

Sara Ahmed, Jane Bennett, Jeffrey Jerome Cohen, Johanna Drucker, Raiford Guins, Graham Harman, renée hoogland, Pam Houston, Eileen Joy, Douglas Kahn, Daniel Miller, Esther Milne, Timothy Morton, Kathleen Stewart, Nigel Thrift, Rob Walker, Michele White.

In association with

BOOKS IN THE SERIES

Bird by Erik Anderson
Blanket by Kara Thompson
Bookshelf by Lydia Pyne
Bread by Scott Cutler Shershow
Bulletproof Vest by Kenneth R. Rosen
Burger by Carol J. Adams
Cell Tower by Steven E. Jones
Cigarette Lighter by Jack Pendarvis
Coffee by Dinah Lenney
Compact Disc by Robert Barry
Doctor by Andrew Bomback
Driver's License by Meredith Castile
Drone by Adam Rothstein
Dust by Michael Marder
Earth by Jeffrey Jerome Cohen and Linda T. Elkins-Tanton
Egg by Nicole Walker
Email by Randy Malamud
Environment by Rolf Halden
Exit by Laura Waddell
Eye Chart by William Germano
Fake by Kati Stevens
Glass by John Garrison
Golf Ball by Harry Brown
Hair by Scott Lowe
Hashtag by Elizabeth Losh
High Heel by Summer Brennan
Hood by Alison Kinney
Hotel by Joanna Walsh
Jet Lag by Christopher J. Lee
Luggage by Susan Harlan
Magnet by Eva Barbarossa
Ocean by Steve Mentz
Password by Martin Paul Eve
Personal Stereo by Rebecca Tuhus-Dubrow
Phone Booth by Ariana Kelly
Pill by Robert Bennett
Political Sign by Tobias Carroll
Potato by Rebecca Earle
Questionnaire by Evan Kindley
Refrigerator by Jonathan Rees
Remote Control by Caetlin Benson-Allott
Rust by Jean-Michel Rabaté
Shipping Container by Craig Martin
Shopping Mall by Matthew Newton
Silence by John Biguenet
Sock by Kim Adrian
Souvenir by Rolf Potts
Snake by Erica Wright
Traffic by Paul Josephson
Tree by Matthew Battles
Tumor by Anna Leahy
Veil by Rafia Zakaria
Waste by Brian Thill
Whale Song by Margret Grebowicz
Bicycle by Jonathan Maskit (forthcoming)
Fat by Hanne Blank (forthcoming)
Fog by Stephen Sparks (forthcoming)
Gin by Shonna Milliken Humphrey (forthcoming)
Office by Sheila Liming (forthcoming)
Pixel by Ian Epstein (forthcoming)
Signature by Hunter Dukes (forthcoming)
Train by A. N. Devers (forthcoming)
Wheelchair by Christopher R. Smit (forthcoming)

snake

ERICA WRIGHT

BLOOMSBURY ACADEMIC
NEW YORK • LONDON • OXFORD • NEW DELHI • SYDNEY

BLOOMSBURY ACADEMIC
Bloomsbury Publishing Inc
1385 Broadway, New York, NY 10018, USA
50 Bedford Square, London, WC1B 3DP, UK

BLOOMSBURY, BLOOMSBURY ACADEMIC and the Diana logo are
trademarks of Bloomsbury Publishing Plc

First published in the United States of America 2020

Cover design: Alice Marwick

Bloomsbury Publishing Inc does not have any control over, or responsibility
for, any third-party websites referred to or in this book. All internet addresses
given in this book were correct at the time of going to press. The author and
publisher regret any inconvenience caused if addresses have changed or sites
have ceased to exist, but can accept no responsibility for any such changes.

Library of Congress Cataloging-in-Publication Data
Names: Badu, Erykah, author.
Title: Snake / Erica Wright.
Description: New York: Bloomsbury Academic, 2020. |
Series: Object lessons| Includes bibliographical references and index. |
Summary: "From Eve to Snakes on a Plane, snakes have seduced and
terrorized humans in equal measure, their mythological status creating real-
world problems for this misunderstood animal"–Provided by publisher.
Identifiers: LCCN 2020009187 | ISBN 9781501348716 (paperback) |
ISBN 9781501348730 (pdf) | ISBN 9781501348723 (ebook)
Subjects: LCSH: Snakes.
Classification: LCC QL666.O6 B155 2020 | DDC 597.96–dc23
LC record available at https://lccn.loc.gov/2020009187

ISBN: PB: 978-1-5013-4871-6
ePDF: 978-1-5013-4873-0
eBook: 978-1-5013-4872-3

Series: Object Lessons

Typeset by Deanta Global Publishing Services, Chennai, India
Printed and bound in Great Britain

To find out more about our authors and books visit www.bloomsbury.com
and sign up for our newsletters.

CONTENTS

Preface xi

1 Kingsnakes and Beauty Queens 1

2 The Problem of the Serpent 9

3 From Mademoiselle Dorita to Britney
Spears: The Snake Charmer Girls 21

4 A Mouse in Your Teeth 31

5 Say Amen and Pass the
Cottonmouth 41

6 Python Pocketbooks 51

7 Who's a Good Boy? 59

8 Snakes Are Not Cheap: Titanoboa and Other Monsters in the Lake 67

9 The Hobbyist 77

10 Sharper Than a Serpent's Tooth 85

11 Magnanimity and True Courage 97

Acknowledgments 111
Notes 113
Index 125

PREFACE

When I was five years old, my family moved into an 1884 Victorian house that had seen better days, the kind of place a real estate agent might describe as having "good bones." And in its state of neglect, critters had moved in. There were mice in the cupboards and squirrels in the attic. During an early walkthrough, my mother found a snake draped casually over the bathroom doorframe. It was a sort of sign. Snakes would continue to be, if not quite a problem, definitely a nuisance for us. Even as my parents improved the place, the snakes never fully vacated. After all, they were there first, had nature's version of squatters' rights.

To be fair, I don't remember the place looking like a house of horrors. I was too young, and by the time I really started forming memories, my parents had put in central plumbing, insulation, air conditioning, and new linoleum in the kitchen. They got one of the fireplaces working and put up wallpaper. And for the most part, the snakes stayed outside. Once when I was in high school, though, I was awakened by a crash downstairs followed quickly by screams and instructions to stay put. A six-foot rat snake had crawled up our dining room mantel and knocked over some candles. I'd like to say we gently corralled it and carried it out the front door to freedom, but that's only true if "freedom" means "the afterlife."

As far as I know, none of our interlopers were venomous. You don't have to be an expert to know your own region's dangerous species, and there are only rattlesnakes, cottonmouths, and copperheads in Tennessee. I saw the occasional cottonmouth, but it was always in the neighbor's creek and never seemed too interested in me. And yet I developed a deep fear of snakes. I would have nightmares about them hiding under my bed. I would run at the sight of a gnarled branch. I would change the channel if *Raiders of the Lost Ark* came on late-night television. Unhealthy, irrational fear. To justify my feelings, I'd say there's something eerie about their silence, the unavoidable sneakiness that comes with slithering. Many people share my sentiments. Some polls suggest that more than half of Americans admit to ophidiophobia.[1] It often ranks higher than fear of public speaking, heights, and spiders.

It's difficult to pinpoint the moment when I decided to immerse myself in snake stories: grandmothers killing copperheads, rock stars injecting themselves with venom, and physicists studying sidewinders. Perhaps it started with my 2013 road trip to the Rattlesnake and Wildlife Festival in Claxton, Georgia, or just as likely with seeing my first anaconda—impossibly large and surprisingly active—at the Tennessee Aquarium. A decade ago, I spent a summer obsessed with Titanoboa, a prehistoric marvel clocking in at around forty feet and weighing over a ton. My childhood was filled with close encounters, and I'm sufficiently embarrassed by the number of times I jumped at discarded snakeskins (or even occasionally a thin stick). I better remember the moment my phobia was pricked with sympathy: watching video footage of rattlesnakes being brutalized for sport at what's called a roundup. I'd never thought much about people killing snakes before, but seeing the animals slaughtered in front of a cheering crowd, hands full of corndogs and hearts full of bloodlust, flipped a switch inside me.

I approached this book with more questions than answers, and let me confess that I am no herpetologist. Only two months before my deadline, I learned snakes don't have eyelids, and I spent the rest of the afternoon in a tailspin, wondering what other basic facts I didn't know. What I do know, however, what interests me the most, is how deeply humans misunderstand the snake. It features prominently in religion, medicine, history, and culture. From the Laocoön to *Snakes on a Plane*, this animal often stands in for fear, and yet its venom has been used to treat heart attacks and has the potential to fight strokes and Alzheimer's. The snake is death and rebirth simultaneously, a crawling contradiction. Popular phrases include "snake in the grass," "lower than a snake's belly," and "a nest of vipers." But on the other side, dreaming of serpents means you're coming into money, and they can be found as representations of power on various flags including the Gadsden ("Don't Tread on Me") and Mexican national. "Snake" can be synonymous with traitor, back-stabber, and villain, but with recent vernacular changes, we can now say danger noodle, nope rope, and snek. As in, that cute snek has a very boopable nose.

One unexpected perk I discovered while writing about this topic is that people are eager to share. Snakes inspire all manner of anecdotes. When I first moved to Atlanta after thirteen years in New York City, I committed to making new friends, but for some reason, I couldn't stop talking about roundups. I had learned too much about these events, and it was as if I had some sort of compulsion to mention beauty pageant contestants dipping their hands in rattlesnake blood, anywhere I went. A few strangers were curious, but many more were simply polite about it. On the other hand, a book about snakes more broadly? People wanted to talk. In the country, locals mention finding them in garages or wood piles. In the city, there are rumors of exotic species finding their way into apartment building toilets. A surprising number of folks caught garter snakes and put them in fish tanks when they were kids. Every tidbit reaffirmed that I'm not alone in my fear or in my fascination.

Newspapers are filled with reptilian fodder, and friends send me their favorites. Commuters in Copenhagen once refused to board a bus that sported a realistic-looking boa constrictor for an ad campaign. A spotted python hitched a ride on an overseas flight by hiding in a passenger's suitcase. A mangrove snake escaped from the Bronx Zoo. I've been sent a documentary from the 1960s on a so-called "signs following" Pentecostal church in West Virginia and an article about a decapitated rattlesnake almost killing someone. On one memorable day, six people sent me links to a story about a "virgin birth," an anaconda at the New England Aquarium having two babies even though she had never mated. All of which is to say, there's an embarrassment of riches in terms of material, and I tried to focus on the subjects I thought would be most compelling, from Britney Spears's famous performance with an albino Burmese python to impressive conservation efforts currently being tackled throughout the world. This book explores both the outsized power and outsized stigma assigned to an animal more likely to hide from humans than to harm us.

Quiet, sleek, alert—the snake is unique and beautiful, a natural marvel that I've come to believe deserves our admiration. Their scales can achieve perfect camouflage or display such vivid hues that it's immediately obvious why dragons continue to capture our collective imagination. Here are little dragons, not flying above our heads, but exploring the world at our feet. If you are someone like me who shivers or sometimes even shrieks when one crosses your path, I hope your initial reaction can also be followed by a sense of wonder. After all, if vipers can change their colors, why can't humans change their minds?

1 KINGSNAKES AND BEAUTY QUEENS

Thirteen-year-old Boyd Fortin holds up a rattlesnake's partially disemboweled carcass, the creature's organs spread like a clothesline across a once-white apron. Richard Avedon photographed the teenager in 1979 at the annual rattlesnake roundup in Sweetwater, Texas, an event that celebrated its sixty-second year in March. At these roundups, wranglers capture thousands of rattlers and bring them to an arena where they are brandished, mutilated, milked, sold, slaughtered, and skinned. Shortly after I moved to Atlanta, someone informed me that Georgia still hosts a yearly roundup, too. "They even crown a beauty pageant queen," I was told. "She kills the first snake."

I started an electronic file called "Roundup Research," but it contains only one document: a link to a CNN video about Sweetwater, which does indeed show pageant contestants.[1] The 2011 winner of the Miss Snakecharmer contest, Laney Wallace, remarks, "Tomorrow I get to skin snakes and chop their heads off, and I'm super excited about it." In another scene, a man squeezes a decapitated snake until its blood drips into a young lady's upturned palms. She turns to a white wall to leave her handprints. That macabre ritual did it for me; a roundup was not in my future. Something about the events still preoccupied me, though, perhaps because I had assumed Avedon's photograph belonged to a time long past, a historical document of a bleaker era. I'm still not sure what I hoped to find at the 2013 Rattlesnake and Wildlife Festival, but it was only a three-hour drive away in Claxton, Georgia, and I talked a friend, high school teacher Kristen Linton, into going with me.

Until 2011, this festival was also a roundup, but the Claxton Chamber of Commerce—responding to concerns from groups such as One More Generation and the Georgia Department of Natural Resources— turned it into an appreciation weekend. At the version Kristen and I attended, few remnants of the festival's gory past remained, but one booth displayed an array of animal pelts for children to stroke, and I nearly bumped into a carton of cottonmouths while trying to snap a photo of tiara-wearing girls posing with a diamondback. Mostly, though, the event was an excuse for families to enjoy a warm spring day and eat fair food. Kristen and I snacked on fried pickles and looked for the conservation booths.

The best of these was The Orianne Society, a non-profit founded to save threatened reptiles and amphibians. I chatted with a herpetologist as he gently maneuvered a Central American indigo for a small crowd. Another scientist approached to show me a scarlet kingsnake, a slim species that grows to only a foot or two in length. "She just shed her skin," the handler said. "That's why she's so glossy." And she was. Her black stripes were iridescent, and I almost wanted to touch them. I surprised myself by admiring what had most scared me as a child. Was this what I had hoped to find? Watching the kingsnake glint in the afternoon light, my only sensation was wonder.

The highlight of the second annual Rattlesnake and Wildlife Festival—for me at least—had nothing to do with snakes. It was a raptor demonstration led by Steven Hein of the Center for Wildlife Education at Georgia Southern University. The hawks, falcons, and owls ate out of Hein's hand and swooped over the crowd of attentive listeners. The message was simple: with contact comes understanding. Hein wants people, particularly children, to have first-hand experiences with wildlife. Nearly every wildlife educator I've met mentions the curiosity of children outweighing apprehension. Recently I spoke with Mike Clifford who leads the education committee for the Virginia Herpetological Society. His own history with reptiles goes back to his childhood, and he gave his first live-animal presentation in high school as part of a science fair (where he reportedly lost and never found his rat snake). A few years later, while taking a public speaking course at Virginia Tech, he brought in a northern water snake, and his instructor climbed onto a desk at the back of the classroom. I've found similar patterns with other reptile enthusiasts—not the scaring-professors part, but the early interest part.

Clifford and I talked about an issue that remains nebulous to me. Is fear of snakes innate or learned? There's data to support both sides of this debate. When shown photographs of snakes, infants' pupils will dilate, implying fear.[2] On the other hand, I've attended plenty of live-animal presentations, and kids tend to be either excited or inquisitive. It's their parents who are more likely to hang at the back. Clifford often presents to younger audiences and confirmed my observations. He also recalled his own early years during which older children would tell him that snakes couldn't be killed, that if cut in two, they would simply grow back together. Even at a young age, his neighbors had been taught superstitions rather than facts.

In a documentary about Avedon from PBS's *American Masters* series, Avedon states, "I think I have photographed what I was afraid of."[3] And a few minutes later: "By photographing what I was afraid of, I explored and learned and laid the ghost." When I flip through my own snapshots of the Wildlife and Rattlesnake Festival, I'm amazed anew by how beautiful that kingsnake is, how docile the eastern indigo, and even how bold the diamondback. The festival may have been partly an excuse to sell crafts and fried foods, but I did gain a new appreciation for both rattlesnakes and wildlife. Which is to say, the event is appropriately advertised.

In the small town of Cocullo, Italy, every May 1st marks a special occasion: Festa dei Serpari. The Serpent Festival. In the weeks leading up to this day, handlers begin catching nonvenomous specimens to drape on the statue of San Domenico di Sora. The ritual is intended to protect residents from dental problems and—appropriately enough—snakebites. While experts may be in charge of the animals, photos from the event show happy children and adult attendees holding them as well. It feels like a magic trick: A sleight of hand and suddenly the evil snake is replaced by the good one. The contrast between a roundup and this festival couldn't be more striking. It's all about spin, albeit in the case of Festa dei Serpari, spin that goes back centuries.[4]

While now a Catholic celebration, it's thought to pre-date Christianity when ancient people of the area worshipped Angitia. (You may not have heard of her, but perhaps you are familiar with her sisters

Circe and Medea.) Angitia was above all a goddess of healing, and snakes in general have a long history of being associated with medicine. Consider the rod of Asclepius, which graces hospitals and doctors' offices throughout the world. Of course, there are plenty of positive superstitions about snakes. I was told as a child that dreaming about them means you're coming into money. There's also the omen that one crossing your path means your luck is about to change (you are soon to become renewed in some way). If you're bitten and survive, you'll supposedly live until a ripe old age as a reward.

While several species are used in Cocullo, the most common type seems to be a striped beauty with golden undertones, the four-lined rat snake. Who knows what the animals think about this affair, but they are treated well, fattened up beforehand with a diet of eggs and mice, then retrieved by their handlers after the festival to be released into the wild.

Another exuberant serpentine celebration happens annually in Manitoba, Canada. Each spring some 70,000 red-sided garters emerge to mate, and intrepid tourists come to watch the spectacle. The otherwise sleepy town of Narcisse bustles with human and serpent activity for a few days.[5] There's also Nag Panchami, a Hindu celebration of the serpent god where worshippers offer milk to cobras but also kill them, not so far removed from our roundups here in the States.

On the drive back from the Rattlesnake and Wildlife Festival to Atlanta, Kristen and I passed the time with the Proust Questionnaire on the back page of *Vanity Fair* and then wrote twenty questions of our own. "How would you least like to die" was at the top of our list. "Being impaled," Kristen answered without hesitation, describing semi-trucks carrying steel beams, the way they could crash through a windshield into her torso. I took a minute to consider. In the past, my answer would have been snake-related, perhaps circumstances akin to the scene from *Raiders of the Lost Ark* when Indiana Jones drops into the pit. As a kid, I never made it past that point in the movie.

I still don't wish to be lowered into the middle of a rattlesnake roundup arena, but when I think of those pens—thousands of creatures with no hope of escape—I feel more sadness than terror. At the end of the day, humans are the most dangerous animal, and we should take responsibility for our outsized fears. The first step might be finding a way to admire what frightens us in nature. "Rotting," I finally answered. Is there a festival for that?

2 THE PROBLEM OF THE SERPENT

Debbie Richards had a new Shi Tzu puppy that snuck out of the house and bounded, as puppies are wont to do, into trouble. The dog's barking caught her owner's attention, and Debbie quickly found her along with a four-foot eastern diamondback. Rattlesnakes are common in Lamesa, Texas, so she didn't panic but instead scooped up her pet and told her husband Milton who said he'd take care of the problem. He found a shovel, then watched the distinctive, alarming tail of the visitor disappearing underneath their deck. He reached out with the shovel, planning to pull the snake toward him and kill it. That's where things went wrong.

Rattlesnakes are venomous pit vipers with a wide range in the United States, though they are especially common in dry, warm locations of the Southwest. Like most snakes, they don't go looking for trouble with humans, but they will defend themselves. As the Department of Wildlife Ecology & Conservation at the University of Florida assures us, you're much more likely to be struck by lightning. In fact, you're more likely to die from a spider bite.[1] (In case you were thinking of sleeping ever again.) Our fear of snakes is out of proportion to the actual damage they can cause, especially considering that there are more nonvenomous than venomous varieties, and they all play an important role in our ecosystems—most notably keeping down rodent populations, preventing the spread of disease. However, second-guess their deadly potential at your own risk.

I grew up in rural Tennessee where from an early age I knew the dangerous types native to my area. Although I spotted a few cottonmouths—what we called water moccasins—at the nearby creek, I never had any run-ins with the others. I was lucky. Left to my own devices, there was little I enjoyed more than exploring my neighbor's big barn where he stored hay for his cows. Despite my luck, I would scream in terror when I inevitably ran across a rat snake. I don't remember a time when I was ever not afraid of snakes—it almost seemed bred into me.

Fear of reptiles actually ranks higher than fear of public speaking, even though a fair number of people have never seen a snake in real life.[2] And while the designation "reptile" covers a range of animals, I don't think anyone's getting worked up over a box turtle. Perhaps more surprisingly, ophiophobia might be evolutionary. A recent study found that infants' pupils dilate when shown images of snakes, an indication of stress.[3]

This study surprised me, but upon reflection, it makes sense: For starters, it matched my own childhood experiences. And while we now have access to life-saving medicines, a bite a million years ago—or even a couple hundred—would have left someone dead. Perhaps this is why they are so often depicted as evil in folklore and religious texts. A natural enemy—or, in a different light, an easy target.

When Milton Richards—who is my first cousin once removed—tried to pull the diamondback from underneath his deck, he quickly realized his mistake. The snake was not in fact moving underneath the wooden planks but up the nearby latticework, disappearing into some ivy. It turned and struck Milton in the hand, puncturing his palm and index finger; he had time to tell his wife before he lost consciousness. Debbie and her son who lives nearby got Milton to the hospital where he was pumped full of antivenin, but still his organs began to shut down, not one by one but several at once. And so began the mystery of what had actually bitten Milton. While certainly dangerous, the eastern diamondback's bite is treatable, and effects are typically not as severe—or as fast—as Milton experienced. Could he have been attacked by the more lethal Mojave rattlesnake? Mojaves aren't native to Lamesa but are typically found farther west in Texas. Could they have migrated or been accidentally transported into the area?

After receiving around forty-eight vials of antivenin, Milton stabilized though doctors remained concerned. Friends and family members began to fill the waiting room, worried that they might need to pay their last respects. Milton himself doesn't remember anything from the first five or six days, but would be released after eight. His relief was short-lived: His second hospitalization quickly followed and lasted more than a month.

Snake identification is an intense hobby, one taken quite seriously by its practitioners. I joined one group on Facebook with more than 100,000 members and strict rules. After someone posts a photo, enthusiasts weigh in, but I use the term "weigh in" loosely. Guesses are absolutely verboten; the latest set of rules warns that violators can be expelled. "There are plenty of experts here," they state. "[W]e will not miss a few." Only species identification is allowed (English and Latin), and conversations are directed toward a sister educational group that has its own rules about jokes and controversial topics (such as cats). The advice for all snakes is to leave them be and, if you suspect the animal might be venomous, a spray of water is recommended. I've lost hours scrolling through the photographs, reading the impressively fast and accurate identifications. Photos that would have once give me nightmares became fascinating, and it's remarkable how our bodies—our reactions—can change through conditioning. Several fellow members report the same phenomenon; after only a few days, they're less scared (or not scared at all). Last year, a seventy-two-year-old woman went viral for killing eleven copperheads who had nested under her Oklahoma home.[4] In the widely circulated photo, she's waving cheerfully at someone off-camera, cup of coffee in the other hand. The very embodiment of sangfroid.

Besides a few lingering effects, Milton feels healthy now and is disinclined to move out of the country as his wife initially wanted. Since being bitten, he's killed thirty rattlesnakes on his property, and he mentions this casually, unimpressed with himself. It's "just a way of life." He remembers being out with his brother when they were kids, playing on a hay bale. They spotted a rattlesnake and trapped it in a thermos to bring home and keep as a pet in their empty fish tank. They tended to the animal until it mysteriously "died" while they were at camp. (Their mother—one of my favorite relatives with a vibrant, confident personality to match her vibrant, confident wardrobe—wasn't as fond of their guest as her boys.) When we talk, Milton seems delighted by this childhood memory, unbothered by his later experience.

The mystery of what variety of rattler bit him lingers, though Milton is somewhat reluctantly convinced the snake was an eastern diamondback that had recently given birth, which would explain the quantity of venom he received from a single bite. Pregnant snakes do not eat, so they are more likely to release all of their venom. On the other hand, there have been upticks of large animal deaths in Lamesa, including a couple of horses and a bull, all of which should have survived with standard veterinarian care. It's possible that a 2011 drought had unintended consequences in terms of the Mojave rattlesnake's range. Farms had to import hay from other parts of the state, and the bales could have served as modern-day Trojan horses. Or the Mojaves could have hitched rides on the pallets brought in from oil fields. Another possibility is that local rattlesnakes are interbreeding with sand varieties. The lack of certainty doesn't seem to worry Lamesa residents too much, though. They are accustomed to cohabitation with dangerous animals. And perhaps their calmness intrigues me the most. The way residents take their serpent neighbors in stride while people—like myself—who have never been in harm's way get the heebie-jeebies thinking about a set of fangs.

In *Paradise Lost*, the poet John Milton retells the story of Eden, how a serpent tricked (or seduced) Eve into eating from the tree of life. It's an oft-told tale and gives some people an easy excuse to consider the snake to be evil. After all, it's biblical. Without the silver-tongued serpent, we could all be living in a sort of heaven on earth, blissed out on ignorance, never knowing pain and never dying. Milton, however, seems sympathetic to the serpent in his verse, repeatedly emphasizing that he was inhabited by Satan, not acting freely when he tempted Eve. The Son of God character speaks plainly on the subject: "Conviction to the Serpent none belongs."[5] The animal is also described as being quite the beauty:

> […] his Head
> Crested aloft, and Carbuncle his Eyes;
> With burnisht Neck of verdant Gold, erect
> Amidst his circling Spires, that on the grass
> Floated redundant: pleasing was his shape,
> And lovely, never since of Serpent kind
> Lovelier

Milton creates a contrast between pretty and ugly snakes (like the kind Satan and his minions become later in the story). It's hard not to draw a comparison between nonvenomous and venomous varieties. Why should the indigo be beheaded for the "sins" of the copperhead?

As Professor Sarah R. Morrison asks in her essay "The Accommodating Serpent and God's Grace in

Paradise Lost," "[if] the serpent is—rather than a corrupt and corrupting influence in the Garden—an unwitting victim and the guilt entirely Satan's, why was the serpent punished?"[6] She argues that Milton highlights the contradictory nature of the serpent in pagan as well as Christian traditions, pointing out that while snakes are associated with Satan (a symbol) they are also of course part of nature (real). The snake also seems to represent the phallic and the feminized at once. I'll add that it's no coincidence that Milton refers to both the snake and Eve as "lovely" in Book 9 when there are a whole host of adjectives available. Morrison continues, pointing out that "just as the alternative of a Serpent beautiful and good as are all the other animals is offered by the text, so too are suggestions of the Serpent's special association with divine wisdom and power. Such conflicting signals point throughout to the problem of the serpent." Her phrase "the problem of the serpent" sticks with me because I know, of course, that snakes aren't evil, no more than sharks or wolves or mosquitos.

Contemporary poet Lucille Clifton goes a step farther in her sequence "brothers," which consists of eight poems in the world-weary (universe-weary?) voice of Lucifer. Clifton humanizes an older, wiser Satan who reminiscences about nature's original beauty. The first poem begins with a retelling of the Garden of Eden story, as well. Lucifer proclaims himself "less snake than angel" and asks, "how come i to this / serpent's understanding."[7] The snake here embodies wisdom, is—like the tree of life itself—the knowledge of good and evil. Indeed, the sequence begins with an invitation to God, "come coil with me," as if the Heavenly Father is as much a snake as the devil himself. Good and evil, as well as their representations here on earth, are sometimes indistinguishable, a wash of gray rather than black and white.

Despite their reputation, snakes are also not widely dangerous in the United States. The Centers for Disease Control and Prevention (CDC) estimates that around 7,000 to 8,000 people are bitten by venomous snakes each year, though less than 0.007 percent actually die from their injuries.[8] And yet one nearly killed my kin. I spoke with Cousin Milton first, but he referred me to his wife for the whole story. He was missing days and knew Debbie would be able to provide a more accurate retelling of his attack and hospitalization. She told me about the way her adult Rottweiler leaned, shaking, on her legs as she went to look for her new puppy. She told me about how the rattlesnake looked green, as if she had recently shed her skin. How after Milton was struck, he declined with alarming speed. And when his arm swelled all the way to his shoulder, she wondered "How tight can your skin get?" Debbie is emotional recalling how her husband's limbs went stiff and his head rolled back after he got into their pickup truck. Still, she tells me that he was fortunate. A young man working an oilfield in Pecos, Texas died a week before Milton's encounter when the medevac helicopter couldn't find him.

In general, there's been an uptick in rattlesnake sightings in the Lamesa area, a phenomenon she speculates as being related to the increased number of oilfields and accompanying development. When snake catchers are trying to flush out a nest, they shake the ground, and there's been an awful lot of rumbling lately. Texas has always been popular with reptiles, but something new is happening in the region. Human tampering with nature rarely ends well.

A man who works for the Richards family was able to find and kill the snake that got Milton. She hadn't gone far. The Richards intended to take her to their local vet to find out more about why her bite was so unusually powerful, but by the time they returned to get her body, it was gone. Most likely, a coyote or hawk had an easy meal. They did, however, perhaps find some of her babies. About a week after Milton got home from the hospital, Debbie was sitting in her car when the smallest rattler she's ever seen—about eight inches long—crawled into the garage and coiled itself into a corner. Milton came out in his bare feet to help, Debbie tells me, laughing a little. "I could have killed him."

An unexpected silver lining of their experience is that their neighbors have been more cautious. One farmer recalls checking his irrigation system, something he'd done a hundred times before, and pausing before opening the instrument panel. Because of Milton's story, he decided to use a shovel instead of his hands, and sure enough, a diamondback was curled inside.

After we get off the phone, Debbie sends me a photograph of a bull snake in their yard. While not likely to win any beauty pageants, it's a big, sturdy fellow that Debbie doesn't mind. She suspects the same snake has been visiting their house lately, a sort of feral pet. While they don't eat rattlesnakes, bull snakes do help keep down the rodent population, which encourages venomous species to hunt elsewhere. Milton is in the photo, too, smiling and healthy. Only their Rottweiler looks skeptical, perhaps wondering if there aren't advantages to being a city dog after all.

3 FROM MADEMOISELLE DORITA TO BRITNEY SPEARS: THE SNAKE CHARMER GIRLS

In 2001, Disney Mouseketeer turned pop sensation Britney Spears strutted out of a cage and onto the stage of MTV's Video Music Awards, wearing a pseudo belly-dancing outfit and singing her hit "I'm a Slave 4 U." While her bedazzled costume and dance moves (to say nothing of one remarkably calm tiger) are memorable, this performance remains a cultural touchstone for one seven-foot, yellow-and-white-scaled beauty named Banana. At about the halfway mark, Britney took the adolescent Burmese python from another performer, carefully draping it over her shoulders and supporting its weight with her hands. For the next minute, she kept the snake stable as she twirled and gyrated then passed Banana to another handler. Even before the snake came front and center, the choreography paid homage to serpent charmers of the carnival circuit. Britney and her backup dancers used a variety of hip movements, including wheels and shimmers along with winding wrist movements to match their scarf accessories. While nobody's denying that it was a singular performance, Britney was participating in a well-established practice.

Snake charming is a traditionally masculine pursuit, a folk art dating back more than a thousand years. You may have seen the practice in person (though it is becoming increasingly rare) or in images: a man sits cross-legged in front of a basket out of which a king cobra appears to sway in time with music from a flute. Snakes, however, do not have ears, and according to Kartrick Satyanarayan, co-founder of Wildlife SOS (along with Geeta Seshamani), they stay focused on the instrument because they see it as a threat.[1] While it seems like a risky pursuit, the charmers are rarely in danger, having removed their animals' fangs or even sewn shut their mouths. Wildlife SOS is currently trying to curb these practices. Although it is illegal to keep a snake in India (where the tradition is most heavily rooted), some skirt the laws. Wildlife SOS wants to convert previous charmers into catchers, seeking their help in removing venomous species from populated areas and releasing them into the wild. India accounts for more than half of worldwide snakebite deaths; Satyanarayan argues that wildlife education can prevent many of these. His organization operates 24-hour reptile-rescue hotlines in three states.

While an old man capable of hypnotizing serpents is one form of charming, Britney represents a more recent development that includes just as much swagger and a lot more exposed skin. Belly dancing was introduced to the United States in 1893, at the Chicago Columbian Exposition. As you might imagine, the performers shocked some audience members; others, presumably, were impressed, given how the practice embedded itself into US culture. (You can now take "Belly Dancing for Beginners" at gyms around the country.) Snake charmers became a popular circus side show. Any operation worth its snuff had one, alongside a bearded lady, a giant, and a sword swallower. There was the Mexican Rattlesnake Queen, Mademoiselle Dorita, Miss Maxine, and the duo Margot and Jenny. The protagonist of Steph Post's novel *Miraculum* is one named Ruby who performs with a 1920s traveling carnival. I asked Post about her research, and she mentioned a snake charmer who was afraid of her own animals, another who used ether to keep her co-stars subdued, and finally the infamous Nala Damajanti who treated her snakes as pets, giving them a bath each Sunday then tenderly wrapping them in towels. Rousseau's painting *La Charmeuse de serpents* combines histories, featuring a naked woman surrounded by snakes—one draped casually over her shoulders—playing a flute.

The hypersexualized snake charmer (primly dressed Miss Uno notwithstanding) points to a conundrum about how we view serpents. In folklore, they are less likely to be feared for their fangs than for their tongues—that is, for their powers of deception or seduction. While Shakespeare's "serpent's tooth" line might be more quoted, in *A Midsummer Night's Dream,* Puck thanks the audience for letting the players "'scape the serpent's tongue." (Nobody hissed at them.) It recalls Margaret Atwood's famous conclusion: "Men are afraid that women will laugh at them. Women are afraid that men will kill them." How appropriate then that the snake represents both sides of this equation. The rattlesnake on the Gadsden flag, coiled above the words "Don't Tread on Me," clearly conveys violence, while Banana being carted around a stage in front of cheering, adoring fans means desire. The snake is both killer and seductress, fangs and forked tongue at once. While visually the python is phallic, it is often associated with women because—as the logic goes—they are desirable but also conniving. Why are snake charmers from nineteenth-century

Zoe Zobedia to twenty-first-century Britney so sexualized? Because we're afraid of female sexuality. Avedon claimed to photograph what scared him the most, so consider one of his most iconic images: actress Nastassja Kinski with a boa constrictor draped across her naked body.

In his exploration of how the West exoticized depictions of snake charming, ethnomusicologist Dr. A. J. Racy describes "a spectacle capable of evoking both interest and repugnance, irresistible curiosity and palpable uneasiness."[2] In fact, his conclusion could be applied to the animal itself, how people around the world are both fascinated and terrified of serpents, a sort of small-scale embodiment of the sublime. Racy concludes that "the snake is said to hold a universal mystique. It is suggested that natural symbols, such as the serpent, are ingrained in our collective psyche." And there does seem to be widespread agreement that the snake represents power, whether positively or negatively.

On every continent save Antarctica, we find the serpent mythologized, mantled with a greater meaning beyond its ecological role. In Madagascar, the Betsileo people believe that their dead can return as snakes.[3] Similarly, Mayan cultures see serpents as symbols of rebirth because they can shed their skins. Fertility, danger, eternal life. Poisonous and healing, the sacred and the profane. It's quite a task, representing good and evil at once, life and death. And that's not even mentioning the gods. In Chinese mythology, we find Nüwa, creator of mankind, who is depicted with the face of a woman and the body of a snake. In Australia, a popular Aboriginal creation story includes the rainbow serpent. In Norse stories, we have Jörmungandr, a giant sea serpent wrapped around the world, poised at any moment to wreak havoc by releasing its tail. The Mesoamerican Quetzalcoatl, the Celtic Bríg, the Minoan Snake Goddess. Shiva is often depicted with an abundance of snakes, and there are too many Greek representations to mention.

It seems we can't get enough of serpents. More than any other animal, this one has captured the human imagination, from ancient superstitions to modern ones. Racy concludes, "the snake appears to embody the ideological link between the past and the present, the distant and the near, the wild and the tame."[4] (He also notes that the combination of snake charming and belly dancing is a decidedly Western invention.) Which is to say, maybe it's a good thing that Britney carried Banana, albeit briefly. Pythons have been carrying their fair share of cultural weight for tens of thousands of years.

Britney's belly-dancing costume was recently auctioned along with her Atelier Versace dress from a different awards show and Levis from the video for "Overprotected (Darkchild Remix)." The whole collection was listed on eBay for a hair under $100,000.[5] The popularity of these memorabilia comes as no surprise: The triple-threat singer-dancer-actress is one of the most recognizable figures in the world. Her most iconic look might be one of her first: the school uniform she wore (collared shirt tied to expose her midriff) in the music video for "Baby One More Time." It's an overtly sexualized portrayal of a Catholic school girl, squarely marketed to teenage girls. Reportedly, the video concept was Britney's idea. She imagined a scenario that resonated with fans—being bored in school and wanting to have fun instead.[6] Of course, this isn't the only example of sexualizing underaged girls. In 1999, the same year that Britney's debut album ...*Baby One More Time* was released—and I graduated high school—we had Wet n Wild lipstick, CK One, and *Beverly Hills 90210*. I never played the popular boardgame Girl Talk: Date Line, but I did own something called Heartthrob. If I remember correctly, for each turn, three photos of men (teenage boys?) were drawn, then in a separate stack of cards each potential date was assigned characteristics such as "Captain of the Football Team" or "Sleeps with a Teddy Bear." While I don't remember the exact wording, one card included something like "Has a Pet Snake," the implication being that for some players a snake in a terrarium is a complete deal breaker.

At the National Museum of American History, you can see a variety of popular board games as well as gowns worn by US first ladies throughout the years. There's Jacqueline Kennedy's yellow silk Oleg Cassini, Nancy Reagan's beaded James Galanos, Barbara Bush's velvet Arnold Scaasi, Michelle Obama's off-shoulder Jason Wu, and Mamie Eisenhower's rose-tinted ("Mamie pink") Nettie Rosenstein, among others. The exhibition begins with Caroline Scott Harrison's luxurious velvet and satin getup and is shortly followed by Eleanor Roosevelt's simple crepe number designed by Sally Milgrim. The Roosevelt includes a caption about the First Lady's approach to fashion: "Understanding that 'busy people like to buy their clothing ready made,' the first lady promoted ready-to-wear clothing but cautioned against buying goods made in sweatshops." Roosevelt wasn't the only one to make political statements with her attire. Lou Henny Hoover favored cotton dresses as a way to support the textile industry. According to Booth Moore in the *Los Angeles Times*, "Lady Bird Johnson sponsored the first White House fashion show to draw attention to the environment and promote travel in America." And even Martha Washington encouraged citizens to buy clothes made in the US.[7]

As the exhibition overview states, "Not all first ladies have popularized fashion, but they have all had their wardrobes scrutinized by the American public." We even have a cutesy name for judging the choices of public figures: fashion police. Lately there's been some pushback against that ubiquitous red-carpet question, "Who are your wearing?" (and pushback against the pushback), but plenty of snark abounds online and in entertainment magazines. Even more concerning, women's clothing is used to determine if assault victims were "asking for it." Recently, the mother of two Notre Dame students wrote a letter to the school paper condemning leggings, urging young ladies to "think of the mothers of sons." In 2017, during a scorching hot summer here in DC, reporters were barred from the House lobby for wearing sleeveless dresses, never mind that the shift has long been a staple of a woman's professional wardrobe. Imagine, bare shoulders as a scandal in a cosmopolitan twenty-first-century city! It would be laughable if it weren't so commonplace. There's a whole spectrum of insults from "slutty" to "prudish," a minefield of possible missteps for girls aged ten and up. I once witnessed a teenager in a school uniform not so far removed from the one Britney wore laying into a man for catcalling her young sister (also in a school uniform).

There's a striking contradiction between society's obsession with the virginal girl—pure of mind and body—and its overt push to sexualize that very image as early as possible. It's as if every woman is a symbol, a sort of Eve figure who is at once the mother of all mankind and its destroyer. Similarly, the serpent is worshipped and condemned, admired and feared. Is Britney's performance remembered because the audience was afraid or mesmerized by the python? Were ticket holders screaming and running from Barnum and Bailey's tents or were they lined up to see Miss Maxine and her bevy of reptiles? We're fascinated by what scares us the most, repelled and drawn in simultaneously. The Snake embodies this dichotomy, even while snakes themselves simply want to go on with their snaky lives, unconcerned with the conundrums of humans, unconcerned with humans at all unless cornered and attacked—or carted around a stage.

4 A MOUSE IN YOUR TEETH

About a month after my sixth birthday, my family decided to spend a weekend camping at a nearby lake, and they persisted with this plan even after some clear warning signs. I can imagine my gleeful, young parents excited about the possibility of swims, sunsets, and s'mores. At the time, my main interest was My Little Ponies, but my brother has always been something of an adventurer, so I'm sure it seemed like a good idea. On Friday afternoon while my father was out getting supplies, our series of unfortunate events began with a long, sleek black snake cornering our cat on the back porch: Picture Delacroix's *Tiger and Snake* except with a house cat and country critter. There was a lot of hissing involved. Neither animal could be quickly convinced to run away despite our best efforts (shrieks). The cat had recently given birth and while the kittens were nowhere in sight, her maternal instincts had kicked in and she was prepared to fight to the death. The snake? I'm really not sure what its problem was, but eventually we (my brother) managed to scare off our intruder.

While one of my goals with this book is to challenge superstitions, we probably should have taken that snake for the sign it was and stayed home. But no, we set up camp at Normandy Lake where a few hours later we watched a man accidentally set himself on fire while trying to light a grill. He ran screaming toward the water, body aflame, before finally submerging and saving himself. After an ambulance came and went, we tried to settle down only to discover that my throat hurt and I was lethargic. I had scarlet fever. We left before nightfall.

I don't remember my illness nearly as much as I remember the snake or man on fire, but I know I had to stay as still as possible for many weeks lest I damage my heart, a poet's childhood to be sure. I didn't realize until I was an adult that scarlet fever is a bit of an antiquated disease, a Victorian calamity that took two of Charles Darwin's children. For me it was a protracted sickness, a bedridden malaise, but thanks to modern medicine, I survived with no as yet discovered side effects besides, perhaps, a heart murmur. If I were a precocious kid or a lying adult, I would say that I remember another sign that the family weekend was doomed: the caduceus on the side of the ambulance. You've seen it before, a winged staff with two intertwined snakes. It's said to belong to Hermes, and if you're confused about why the messenger of the gods (sometimes known as the god of poetry) would grace hospital entryways, you're not alone. In fact, this symbol is a recent mistake. The real symbol of healing is the rod of Asclepius, which boasts only one snake and no wings.[1] (The cover of Anne Boyer's new memoir *The Undying* has a beautiful, modern rendition.)

How did an animal feared in so many cultures come to be commonly accepted as a medical herald for more than 2,000 years? One explanation is simply that since snakes shed their skin, they suggest new life, another start and another chance. Venomous snakes also carry their own antivenin. That is, they can hurt and heal at once, poison and cure that poison. Always when we start to dive into the symbolism of the serpent, it embodies contradiction more than anything else: light and dark, goodness and evil, wisdom and deception, life and death.

For more than thirty years, rock star and snake enthusiast Steve Ludwin has been injecting himself with snake venom. No, he's not an obscure sideshow freak nor is he exactly a man with a death wish, though it seems like a safe bet to argue that he's cavalier about his own mortality. He looks like a young Stephen Moyer, though Moyer is a couple of years younger biologically. Ludwin seems to have found the fountain of youth, and it's a cocktail of venoms. Step right up for your Gaboon viper face cream. He briefly had his own snake-related show on Vice called *Man and Snake* where he could be found meeting pageant contestants at the rattlesnake roundup in Sweetwater, Texas, and attending worship services at a Pentecostal church in West Virginia.

The term "snake oil" is synonymous with a con of a particular variety, something slick and swathed in pseudo-science. Recent headlines have given the designation to cannabidiol (CBD products), the Second-Act industry, tariffs, neuromarketing, Bernie Sanders, Sarah Sanders, and artificial intelligence. It's a metaphor so embedded in our vocabulary that it's lost all connection to its origins. Those origins, despite popular belief, weren't a ruse at all.

In the 1800s, thousands of Chinese workers arrived in the United States as indentured laborers to help construct the Transcontinental Railroad. They brought with them a homemade remedy for inflammation that they would rub into their joints after a long day. According to reporter Lakshmi Gandhi, their American peers "marveled at the effects." The substance came from the fat of Chinese water snakes, which is rich in Omega 3 acids, and attempts to replicate this elixir with American snakes (such as the rattlesnake) failed.[2] But that didn't stop enterprising and conniving men from hawking their wares across the country. In fact, medicine became its own sort of sideshow.

By all accounts, Ludwin is no snake oil salesmen and genuinely cares about reptiles. In the Vice episode that takes place in a "signs following" Pentecostal church, a preacher can be seen stepping on a cottonmouth, and Ludwin's body language changes. He goes from being a spirited audience member, dancing to the workshop music, to a critic, arms crossed in front of his rigid body. He mouths "animal abuse" to the camera and later tries to reason with the preacher about his behavior. Ludwin certainly does not see the snake as an embodiment of evil, something to be tortured to demonstrate a person's faith. In an interview for *The Guardian*, Ludwin mentions the proliferation of snakes as symbols, highlighting their role in medicine.[3] It's appropriate, of course, that his mind would go there first. Experts at the University of Copenhagen are working to develop a human-derived antivenin using Ludwin's blood. (Antivenins are traditionally created using horse blood.)

He's injected rattlesnake, viper, cobra, and black mamba venoms among many others, often more than one at once. In case you're wondering, yes, he has most definitely been admitted to the hospital before. Multiple times. In a film for the Natural History Museum (UK), Ludwin mentions that early on he was injecting venoms every other day and admits that he didn't know what he was doing. His goal from the beginning was clear, though: to become immune.

And it seems to have worked. Ludwin mentions being grateful that his experiments might help others and concludes that "what can kill you can also save you."[4]

Ludwin credits herpetologist Dr. Bill Haast for giving him the idea that he could become immune.[5] Haast died in 2011 at the age of 100 and estimated that he had handled more than three million venomous snakes. Haast directed the Miami Serpentarium, a snake venom producer in Florida that was also open to the public as a tourist attraction for many years. Known as the Snakeman, Haast the performer was also Haast the savior. He would travel to remote locations to treat snakebite victims with his own blood. Venezuela even made him an honorary citizen when he ventured deep into the jungle to save a young boy. His *New York Times* obituary includes his rueful regret that the snakes were never really pets. It quotes from an interview in *Outside* magazine: "You could have a snake for 30 years and the second you leave his cage door cracked, he's gone. And they'll never come to you unless you're holding a mouse in your teeth."[6]

There are many parallels between Haast's and Ludwin's stories, one of which is an early appreciation of snakes. While it seems that many infants are born with an innate fear of the animal, that evolutionary trait skipped these two men. As children, they both caught snakes, much to the chagrin of Haast's mother. As they got older, their interests turned into obsessions.

Ludwin's former girlfriend (and interviewer for *The Guardian*) Britt Collins recalled their unusual living arrangement when they were attending college: "Our house was a zoo, with our potbellied pig Lou who loved the Velvet Underground, a ginger-and-white rat Moo-Moo whom I saved from the fangs of a copperhead, a pair of rescued iguanas, a vicious baby caiman crocodile and a terrifying assortment of snakes and scorpions."

Currently, there is no synthetic version of antivenin. To create this life-saving drug, a venomous snake must be persuaded to release its venom into a container. The handler grips it behind the head and pushes in such a way that the valuable liquid drips from the fangs. Or, in an updated method, the handler allows the snake to strike a permeable surface. Less than a teaspoon is collected from a single animal.[7] Extractors are cagey about the amount of money they bring in annually, but demand is constant. Most varieties of venomous snake require their own type of antivenin—you can't treat a bite from a coral snake with diamondback antivenin.

In addition to its mythological origins, the snake as a symbol for medicine makes sense practically, as well. Scientists believe that the medicinal potentials of venom are far-reaching. A drug for blood clots created from studies of the saw-scaled viper has been on the market since 1998. Neurotoxins might one day be used to treat brain injuries and Alzheimer's. Some experts believe that we could see snake venom playing a role in treating Parkinson's and breast cancer, as well.[8] A substance that strikes fear into so many hearts could be used to restart those very organs.

That is the contradiction of the snake, a living embodiment of duality. Through this lens—a creature that can take but also give life—it becomes possible to see why humans have elevated it to something more than flesh and blood. By this logic, it must be an extension of God or Satan; it must be otherworldly. And while worship has led to protections in some locations, associations with evil have led to abuses. It sometimes seems as if we are incapable of simple appreciation. We must also own it, make it mean what we want it to mean. Yet the snake resists.

Perhaps in a more optimistic mood, we are not incapable of appreciation, only reluctant. It is difficult to change a mind, but not impossible. While few of us will choose the paths of Ludwin and Haast, we can learn to leave our garden visitors alone. If we do not like their unusual beauty, we can at least like their utilitarian nature. They can keep down vermin populations and even cure diseases. There's more to praise than to censor.

Oceans kill far more humans every year, and yet we return to their threatening beauty. We snap selfies with waves washing ashore behind us and send postcards to our landlocked friends. We shell out for airfare or drive hours to let the tide slip over our feet. Yes, we are capable of admiring nature, however dangerous. We are capable of humility, an understanding that our life is ephemeral, will slip through our fingers like scales. There is no real fountain of youth, only reminders of our own mortality. And in our brief moment on earth, we can choose to destroy or protect. Humans are as contradictory as any animal, as dual-natured, as menacing and as helpful. We hold both the powers of destruction and redemption. And it's up to us to choose.

5 SAY AMEN AND PASS THE COTTONMOUTH

In my senior year of high school, five Tennessee children were orphaned when their preacher father died of snakebites received during a Pentecostal church service. Their mother had been killed in the same manner a few years earlier. While I'm not sure how much national attention the story received, it looms large in my memory, perhaps because of the unbelievable ruling that the paternal grandparents could have partial custody of the children despite the fact that they ran their own serpent-handling church in North Carolina.[1] The grandparents promised not to take the minors to any more services, but even as an optimistic, naïve seventeen-year-old, that promise seemed far-fetched to me. The children themselves had seen such promises broken before: Their own father had been granted custody because of his assurances that he would no longer expose them to venomous snakes. To be fair, the judge didn't have a lot of great options. The maternal grandmother had also once been a serpent-handling participant, though she maintained that was in her past.[2] There's almost a hiss in the air, forked tongues flicking, but coming from human rather than animal mouths. From the outside looking in, these communities feel fueled by addiction as much as by faith.

A 1967 documentary by Peter Adair, *Holy Ghost People*, begins with some light background information about worshippers who are looking for "a direct experience with the holy spirit."[3] At the time, there were about a thousand churches in the US—mostly in Appalachian regions—that included speaking in tongues, faith healing, drinking strychnine, and handling venomous snakes in their services. After interviews with a few members of the congregation, the cameras turn to a service in Scrabble Creek, West Virginia. Perhaps most surprising—at least to me—was the lack of a designated pastor that day. There was no charismatic ringleader, no cult figure conning people into dangerous practices. In fact, the first man to speak comes across as down-to-earth and even a little self-deprecating. He's the older relative you don't mind meeting at your family reunion. Unexpectedly, given the state of the Deep South in the '60s, he speaks bluntly and openly against racism, ending with a nonchalant "everybody's just people." And indeed, while most of the considerable crowd seems to be white (the grainy film makes it somewhat difficult to tell), there are at least a few African American members of the community, one of whom plays the guitar and sings a catchy duet with a young woman later in the service. And speaking of music, it's lively and fun, classic bluegrass. The whole thing comes across as joyful. There's a lot of hugging, dancing, and smiling—it's no wonder the place is packed. Then the venomous snakes arrive, and they are not as lethargic as I am expecting. There are also a lot of them. I have to turn the footage off for a second to let my heart rate slow down.

These signs following Pentecostal churches—not all Pentecostal churches participate in dangerous activities—are not as prolific as they once were, with around twenty-five left. West Virginia is the only state where the practice is legal without any restrictions. In recent footage that aired on Vice for Ludwin's *Man and Snake* show, it's clear to me that these are not your grandparents' snake-handling churches, and to be honest, that's a shame. Instead of the humble, happy sincerity of Scrabble Creek that we see in the 1967 documentary, there's a pastor who sounds like a carnival barker, shouting into an unnecessary microphone.[4] He talks about his drug addiction and how God saved him, which should be uplifting but comes across as aggressive and angry, as if daring someone to disagree with him. The snakes seem like an afterthought as well as drugged, dehydrated, or chilled to the point of near death. The pastor swings one around, its body flopping like a plastic toy. (The same languid body language can be seen in a short film about the church made for West Virginia's *Register Herald*.[5])

I wonder about the churches that don't allow access to reporters, though, the kind I used to hear about growing up, their names whispered rather than shouted—the illegal ones that still exist outside of West Virginia. Are they less spectacle and more authentic? On a Facebook page for serpent handlers, the postings don't look that much different than what you might see from older relatives. Stock photos and inspirational phrases, sometimes well-known scripture passages about love and hope. In one message, a member mentions that a European reporter would like to attend a worship service, and could anyone help? The replies are polite but negative. The general consensus seems to be that journalists have no interest in showing a well-rounded portrait of their Sundays; they're only interested in the snakes. It's a complaint that seems reasonable, Adair's documentary notwithstanding. Some parishioners don't see themselves as that different from the Presbyterians down the street; they just happen to believe a biblical commandment ignored (or interpreted differently) by others.

This practice originates in the book of Mark in which Jesus speaks to his disciples after he has risen from the tomb: "And these signs will accompany those who believe: In my name they will drive out demons; they will speak in new tongues; / they will pick up snakes with their hands; and when they drink deadly poison, it will not hurt them at all; they will place their hands on sick people, and they will get well."[6] Signs followers interpret these predictions literally (that crucial word "shall" a commandment rather than a prophecy) and focus their practices around them. It's an example of cherry-picking Bible verses, an accusation often leveled at Christians who want to make Christianity more inclusive. Members of the LGBT+ community are often told that they are sinners because of a handful of problematic scripture excerpts. The story of Sodom is particularly worrisome because in its supposed condemnation of homosexuality, it endorses rape. Leviticus 18:22 is also a popular excuse for hate and is admittedly explicit: "Do not have sexual relations with a man as one does with a woman; that is detestable."[7] But of course we know that Leviticus is also the book that says a couple that has sex during a woman's period should be outcasts and that a man cannot marry a widow. There are rules on who can attend church services as well as a lot of animal sacrifices. One of the punishments for not following all the myriad rules is that a man will have to eat his own sons and daughters. Which is to say, I don't know a single Christian who doesn't cherry-pick. Why favor the verses that require you to dance with a cottonmouth (or discriminate against anyone)?

Serpents appear throughout the Bible, first in Genesis and last in Revelations. In the middle, we've got the staff of Moses that can turn into a snake to prove the existence of God. When the Israelites grow restless in their exile to the wilderness and turn on Moses, God sends venomous snakes to punish them. In Micah, the threatened punishment is that disbelievers will be turned into snakes, eating the dust below them. In Psalm 58, sinners are compared to cobras who refuse to listen to their charmer. In Matthew, Jesus commands his disciples to "be as shrewd as snakes and as innocent as doves"—hinting at a more positive interpretation of the animal, that its wiles might also be useful.[8] In perhaps a less well-known story than the Garden of Eden, the disciple Paul is shipwrecked on Malta where he is bitten by a viper. The locals think at first that he must be a murderer, but when he survives, they consider him a god instead. He also heals the sick while on the island, harkening back to the signs passage from the book of Mark.

In *Holy Ghost People*, the snakes are brought out in what seem to be velvet bags, then let loose on the floor. Parishioners who feel called to do so may come and hold them; a few move forward, picking them up in a way that looks similar to what you might see at a wildlife show, and I wonder if they've been taught or simply learned through observation. They do dance with them and hold them up, sometimes several at once. At a few key points, the camera cuts to the children at the back as if to remind us that they could be in danger if things get out of control. I think about the Brown children and wish I knew what happened to them. They'd be in their twenties now, perhaps full-fledged members of a congregation or perhaps they managed to leave that life behind. I find no trace of them online.

In West Virginia, children are still allowed to attend these services. To be honest, I had misremembered this law, or never learned it correctly. I thought minors were banned. I suppose I assumed that they would be along the lines of minors being denied entry to bars and R-rated movies. It's hard for me not to view this practice in the lens of exemptions for vaccines, this prizing of the parents' beliefs over the children's well-being. There were quite a few children in attendance at the 1960s Scrabble Creek service, some smiling and some visibly bored. A couple of bouncing babies. I get used to watching the adults hold snakes, and I check the time left on the video. There are only a few minutes left, so I let it play instead of fast-forwarding, which is good because I miss the bite anyway. I rewind and still can't see it, but suddenly a man is holding a handkerchief to his hand and praising God. His only sign of distress at the beginning is a calm statement that he'd "like to know why this happened, he'd like for God to tell him." Part of the tradition mandates refusing medical treatment. Instead, a few people put their hands on him, hoping to heal him. But the crowd gradually grows quieter as the seriousness of the situation becomes apparent. The man hangs his head, and his hand swells. The documentary ends before we learn what happens.

I'm no film critic, but *Holy Ghost People* seems rather remarkable. The focus is on the subjects rather than Adair's point of view, except perhaps for the lingering last shot of the swollen hand, a reminder that these nice people partake in a rather treacherous practice. I was struck by the lack of hubris, though, not just in the director but in the worshippers. It's always seemed a little arrogant to me, this belief that God wants you to not simply be calm if you happen to encounter a snake—that part makes a certain sense—but to willingly put yourself in harm's way, banking on being saved. It reminds me of a Bible verse that a lot of non-Christians can recite: "And now these three remain: faith, hope and love. But the greatest of these is love."[9] That is, faith is important, but it's not everything. You've also got to help (love) others and yourself.

I suppose I was expecting someone to be profiting off of these beliefs, but the packed Scrabble Creek church collects less than $50 (about $350 in today's money). And I doubt the contemporary pastor on the Vice show is getting even that much given the low attendance. It's something besides money that draws folks to this practice. Maybe the constant reminder of the nearness of death makes them more grateful for their lives, more willing to appreciate the joys of daily life. There's a little New Age mindfulness in there, something our celebrity culture and glossy magazines might embrace in a less venomous form. While snakes play a central role in these services, these are not snake-worshipping places. Indeed, it's clear that the serpent is associated with evil as much as with death. You can't help but wish they'd simply let the snakes go—these are no devils in disguise, just animals that would do good and decidedly less harm in their own ecosystems.

There's footage of the Brown children's father being struck by the fatal rattlesnake, as well.[10] The pastor can be seen walking and talking briefly after the injury, reassuring his parishioners that "God's still God, no matter what comes." It only takes about ten minutes for the worship service to turn quiet as the attendees realize that their leader has died. Well, most attendees realize. There's a young girl watching everything with a smile on her face, seemingly unaware of what's transpired, that the adults in the room have failed her in a fundamental way.

6 PYTHON POCKETBOOKS

The logo for Versace's fashion empire is Medusa's head, a woman's face ringed with serpents. Founder Gianni Versace said in interviews that it was inspired by a depiction he encountered as a child in the ruins of Reggio Calabria, a coastal Italian city. The figure of Medusa is well-known, the sort of monster you can't recall first encountering, but by ten years of age you could spot her in a Halloween crowd as easily as you could mark Dracula and Frankenstein's monster. I do remember watching *Clash of the Titans* (1981) as a kid, my young mind impressed by the cleverness of Perseus. Medusa crawls into the scene, hissing (a sort of low growl) while Perseus waits behind a pillar, knowing that if he looks at the creature directly, he will be turned to stone. Instead, he spies on her with his shield as the Laurence Rosenthal score warns us of imminent danger. Medusa is a rattlesnake in this depiction, though surely a cat snake would be more regionally appropriate. Eventually Perseus is able to kill her with a well-timed swing of his sword. The scene is dark and chaotic, and I'm only about 50 percent confident that I'm summarizing the events correctly even after re-watching it as an adult. What's clear, though, is that Medusa should be feared.

Before Medusa was a monster, she was merely a woman whose beauty caught the attention of Poseidon. If you know your Greek mythology at all, you know it rarely ends well when a mortal gets ensnared in the goings-on of the immortals. Poseidon raped Medusa in the temple of Athena, then—in a whopping act of victim blaming—Athena punished Medusa for befouling her temple. She transformed her locks into venomous snakes, and Medusa's head became a weapon, capable of turning someone to stone with a single glance. In Ovid's retelling of her story in *Metamorphoses*, her assassin Perseus sees her kills as he approaches her lair:

> And everywhere, in fields, along the roads,
> he witnessed the sad forms of men and beasts
> no more themselves, but changed now into stone,
> misfortunate, who'd glimpsed Medusa once.
>
> translator, **CHARLES MARTIN**[1]

Perseus doesn't note anything wrong with Medusa being punished for her own assault. Medusa has been rehabilitated by artists over the years, though, starting as early as the fifth century when vases depicted her as the innocent and Perseus as the attacker.[2]

In a dramatic monologue titled "Medusa," poet Patricia Smith reimagines the gorgon as neither victim nor monster, but rather an empowered woman who wanted to sleep with Poseidon: "We defiled that temple the way it should be defiled, / screaming and bucking our way from corner to corner."[3] In this version, Medusa describes her own unexpected bodily changes, her arms burning and scales growing. The surprise of her hair moving. Over the years the myth of Medusa has simplified into three attributes: her beauty, her snakes, and her ability to turn men to stone. Honestly, it's not a bad way to market clothes. I'd be lying if I said there was never a moment that I wanted to turn a leering—or worse—man into some granite.

In early 2018, the Versace company banned the use of fur in their work, but leather is still fair game. There's currently a men's belt with the iconic logo available for $1,750. Pumps, gloves, and a $4,000-dollar jacket. Purses, of course, and a business card holder. A miniskirt and some high-waisted shorts. A $1,000-dollar throw pillow. A baseball cap. Corsets, dresses, and pants. There's no underwear, but if you don't mind going commando, you can clad yourself from head to toe in chic, expensive high-end cowhide.

While they do not currently seem to offer any genuine snake products, python print is an option. And other labels embrace the real deal. In 2017, Kering—which owns Gucci, Alexander McQueen, and Balenciaga among others—created its own python farm in Thailand with the purpose of supplying its brands with skins.[4] Apparently the demand for patterned leather is so high that the unusual move made sense. In a statement, Kering assured investors that the animals would be raised in good conditions before becoming runway wear.[5] Kering also helped found the Python Conservation Partnership, an organization devoted to "the aim of contributing to the improved sustainability of the python trade and helping facilitate industry-wide change."[6]

I grew up near a tannery, and the acrid combination of dead animals plus chemicals would sometimes make me gag, stumbling as quickly as possible from our back door to our car. I can describe days in the country that would make you long for a rural existence. Dramatic pink sunsets over the green horizon, followed by dancing fireflies and eventually a storm of constellations overhead. Grass under your bare feet and honeysuckle filling the air, blackberries ready to be picked in the morning. Other days, the local chicken farms would stir up literal shit, and you could see filth in the air, feel it on your arms and in your eyes. When the chicken farms and tannery kicked up at once, I'd dream of catching the first flight to the nearest big city.

I don't begrudge the farms or the tannery. Jobs were scarce enough in my rural county. But if you don't know anything about how leather turns into a pair of boots, let me tell you—the process isn't pretty. In its history lesson about Jamestown, the National Park Service includes a section on seventeenth-century tanning, referring to the "noxious solutions" used in the process.[7] But "noxious solutions" sugarcoats the eye-stinging stench produced by these operations— which is to say, it's no wonder tanneries are often relegated to the outskirts of town.

While the humans of Florida get the most headlines, the ecosystems are equally surprising and diverse. Reefs, dunes, swamps. Miles of coast and acres of forest. In the panhandle, live oaks teem with Spanish moss, and white sand leads to clear, emerald water. In addition to rollercoasters and princess castles, central Florida boasts natural springs and manatees. And if we continue farther south, we eventually hit the Everglades, marshland famous around the world for its natural treasures, including alligators and even the occasional Florida panther. A new predator arrived in the 1980s, though, and by the early 2000s had started to wreak havoc on native species: the Burmese python. It was once legal to import this animal for the pet trade, and tens of thousands made it into the state, many of which were released into the wild when owners were no longer able or interested in caring for a creature that can grow to twenty feet and weigh two hundred pounds.

The python invasion of southern Florida has been a well-documented catnip for filmmakers and journalists. I'll warn you right now that if you watch one YouTube video of a man wrestling a fifteen-foot snake into a sack, your recommended content will be reptilian for months. But are the trespassers really doing that much damage? The short answer is yes. With no natural predators, the pythons have thrived, breeding at alarming rates. They have devastated small mammal populations and shown up in suburban areas. The longer answer is more complicated, though. Yes, pythons are a problem, but media attention has led to increased funding to curb their domination. Other species haven't been so lucky (or unlucky depending on your outlook). Invasive plants can quietly destroy habitats, cause flooding, and deplete oxygen levels without getting so much as a peep on the nightly news. A top result for "invasive plants" on YouTube ("16 Invasive Species Sold at Garden Centers You Should Never Buy") has a respectable 150,000 views. The top results for "invasive pythons"? On the first page of results alone, there are videos that have 4, 5, and 10 million views respectively.

Efforts to stop the expanding python invasion include a variety of approaches, some of which (like trained canines) have been successful while others (perhaps most notably the amateur week-long python-catching competitions) have been less so. Currently the South Florida Water Management District employs full-time python hunters who are paid $8.46 an hour plus per-snake bonuses.[8] They are allowed to keep the skins to sell for products.

Versace's logo is beautiful, of course, and surprisingly understated for a brand synonymous with vibrant, sometimes garish designs. Versace equals in-your-face luxury. And yet the logo could be drawn with a few strokes of the pen, the snakes implied rather than recreated. There are no fangs or even scales, only serpentine curves. The end result resembles a lovely woman wearing a headscarf rather than a mythological monster. While a wildly popular company (recently acquired by Michael Kors), interest outside the fashion world has recently been rekindled by a Netflix series, *The Assassination of Gianni Versace: American Crime Story*. In 1997, Versace was murdered on the steps of his Miami estate in front of his security gates. In real life, those gates had a pretty but indistinguishable design. In the docudrama version, twin gold Medusas watch over the violence impassively, as if resigned to the world's resentment of anyone singular, anyone defying expectations. They can be seen peering out as fans fill the steps with candles, flowers, and messages in the days following the designer's death. A symbol of a symbol. Versace created his own mythology. How appropriate that he selected such an infamous vixen as the face of his company, moreover a vixen perhaps unfairly—and fatally—misunderstood.

7 WHO'S A GOOD BOY?

At the Temple of Pythons in Ouidah, Benin—a site where the sacred and commercial meet—a hundred or so snakes calmly reside.[1] Visitors can hold the pythons or drape them over their shoulders for photographs. While technically captive, the reptiles are freed at night to hunt for prey, and some end up in nearby homes where residents treat them respectfully and return them, a normal part of life in this West African city. Snakes are sacred in the Vodun, and a rainbow serpent acts as an intermediary between humans and God. Louisiana voodoo has its roots in this religion, and snake iconography can be seen throughout New Orleans, from the Voodoo Museum to the Museum of Art. Don't believe B-horror movies—snakes are seen as symbols of peace and prosperity. Not the devil, but the divine.

There was recently a ball python up for adoption at my local Humane Rescue Alliance. I know because

I used to check the website daily for cats, wondering when I would be ready for another pet. My beloved feline companion of fourteen years had died the previous year. Lola's death was expected, and yet her loss devastated me. I found myself unmoored and not even poetry—my go-to panacea for a broken heart—could provide any comfort. Months later, I found myself staring at Salazar the Snake. He seemed to be smiling for the camera. If I'm being honest, he was much more photogenic than the available cats who often wore wide-eyed, lost expressions, their coats a little mussed, their claws a little out. Salazar looked ready for his *National Geographic* debut, sleek and attentive.

Sometimes I would stare at Lola's green eyes, more specifically at the vertical pupils, and wonder if I would recognize her if she metamorphosed into, say, a pit viper; the eyes of these two creatures can be eerily similar. Perhaps what I was really asking was, what are the strangest forms of love? As Mary Oliver directs us in her poem "Wild Geese," "You only have to let the soft animal of your body / love what it loves."[2]

When I think about Oliver's poetry, I think about standing still, so still and for such a long time that nature settles, forgets an apex predator is in her midst. Oliver is a patient poet, content to ask questions and wait on answers, a quality that poet John Keats would call "negative capability." It's not an easy place to occupy, a humbling, an acceptance of being no better than trees or birds or fish. In "Some Questions You Might Ask," Oliver considers the soul, wondering why she as a human would have one, but not other creatures like anteaters or camels. She also considers what the soul might look like, proposing the feel of iron and the shape of an iceberg. She asks, "Does it have one lung, like the snake and the scallop?" It's such a surprising choice, comparing what is thought to make us immortal with a serpent and a mollusk. Except for pythons and boas, snakes do indeed have only one lung, and it occupies most of their bodies. Imagine, being mostly a breathing machine.

Most pet snakes are non-aggressive, but that doesn't explain the high school kid in Nevada who hid more than forty venomous species, including a Gaboon viper, in his bedroom.[3] What was the appeal? Was he simply captivated by the animals? Did he love them? Was he addicted to the danger? He's certainly not alone. There's a thriving black market for snakes. In 2017, a man was arrested for smuggling—among other reptiles—three cobras into the United States via potato chip cans.[4] And according to Endangered Species International, 3 percent of US households have a pet reptile.[5] That's about four million homes. Of course, that number includes turtles, lizards, and other less stigmatized animals, but it's still impressive.

There are plenty of folks out there who appreciate serpentine beauty.

Snake owners talk about how fascinating they find their pets, that the appeal is something beyond companionship. They also require less care than a cat, dog, horse, or even a bird. One woman I spoke to mentioned being emotionally attached to her California king snake, but she started to become afraid of him after he bit a visitor. A friend of mine had a similar experience with a corn snake, minus the bite. At first enamored, she eventually became fearful, a reverse experience of what you might expect. Exposure therapy has its limits, I suppose.

Locally here in DC, there's a program called "Blue Collar Cats" through the Humane Rescue Alliance where you can apply for an "unadoptable" feline—one they think has no potential to overcome its feral state—that you agree to shelter and feed in exchange for its pest control services. When a friend took one, I thought for sure that kitty would end up inside, snoozing on the couch and occasionally demanding ear rubs. But it's been more than a year, and the cat still hisses when its owner brings out food in the morning. There are four beautiful cats that roam my neighborhood—three orange tabbies and a calico. They will let me pay my respects as long as I stay a few feet away, and I saw them on my walk this afternoon, regally sitting on a neighbor's porch. They're well-cared for, perhaps by that neighbor or several, and they will not let anyone pet them. So it goes with many beautiful creatures in nature.

In my Facebook snake identification group, someone posted a photo of a ringneck in central Texas; it's remarkably pretty. Tiny with a sleek gray back and vivid orange underbelly that is—look it up if you don't believe me—polka-dotted. In the photo, a woman gently cradles it in her hand, and the little guy seems unperturbed.

Efforts are underway to change the image of reptiles. Cute euphemisms like "danger noodles" and "sneks" circulate, and Instagram accounts feature them with tiny accessories such as hats and scarves. When a baby cobra went missing from the Bronx Zoo in 2011, an account with the handle @BronxZoosCobra (affectionately called "Snake on the Town") popped up on Twitter and garnered more than 200,000 followers. The lighthearted account posted about the cobra's imagined escapades, visiting landmarks around New York City. While common pet snake names include the expected Fang and the ironic Fluffy, there's also Fifi the death adder who gave birth at Australia's Featherdale Wildlife Park in 2014. On Instagram under the hashtag #cutesnake, you'll find a corn snake named David Hisslehoff, a western hognose named Lavender, and a ball python named Caper (that looks remarkably like Sir Hiss from Disney's *Robin Hood*). The comments on these photographs are almost entirely enthusiastic. Wildlife educators hope that snake perceptions might be changing.

If you have a pet, I'm sure you can describe the predominant characteristics: loyal, reactive, playful, smart, calm, loathes the poodle next door, loves the dog park. As with people, animals have their own personalities, and we get to know their lovable quirks alongside, say, their refusal to pee if the sky so much as looks like it's going to rain. From this angle, it's not so hard to understand why there are efforts to anthropomorphize reptiles. It's one of many tactics used to convince people with phobias to see them as friends rather than natural enemies—or, if not as friends, as least as useful acquaintances.

I wish this chapter ended with Salazar the Snake hanging out with me on the sofa, watching *Russian Doll*, but instead there's Penny, a beagle mix with liquid brown eyes as far from a pit viper's slits as can be. The good news, though, is that Salazar *was* adopted from the Humane Rescue Alliance. I don't know who brought him home, but I hope they're delighted with their new friend. Now at the shelter there's Fred the corn snake who is not quite as photogenic as Salazar, but he's got pretty copper scales and a sort of sweet expression if you squint. I'm rooting for him, as well. I adopted Penny in part because my friends had adopted a beagle mix from the same shelter. Luna is a regal dog, affectionate but also independent, and I thought that combination would work well for me. While they look quite similar, Penny couldn't be more different from her shelter mate. She is decidedly needy, what vet behaviorists call a Velcro dog because she's always by my side. Predictably, I fell head over heels in love with her, but I wouldn't say she's the dog I thought we were taking home.

It's human hubris to think that we can control animal personalities, that if we breed or train in a certain manner, we can guarantee ourselves a pliable friend. Characteristics are determined by nature, of course, but also nurture—those experiences that create trust or fear, the ones that make a Great Dane try to hide under a bed during a thunderstorm or an alley cat approach a stranger. One domesticated python isn't exactly like the next. This is true of species in the wild, as well. Those tell-tale Hershey kisses on the back of a copperhead? They're not always as obvious as the educational drawings indicate. And an aggressive racer might have a shy sibling hiding somewhere nearby. While putting a unicorn horn on a snake doesn't give it a personality, the Instagrammers might be onto something. The more human we imagine a creature, the less likely we are to harm it. The next time you're startled by a nope rope in your yard, perhaps you can appreciate the remarkable way it moves without limbs or even the way its mouth quirks up in what could be called a smile with a certain stretch of the imagination. Instead of a shovel, you can reach for a water hose and suggest it exit the way it came. After all, it could be someone's pet death adder named Fifi.

8 SNAKES ARE NOT CHEAP: TITANOBOA AND OTHER MONSTERS IN THE LAKE

I first read about a prehistoric giant snake—more than forty feet long and weighing in at a ton—while doing my laundry in a damp basement of Washington Heights. Someone always left behind their old issues of *Smithsonian Magazine*, and I always read them. The discovery of *Titanoboa cerrejonensis* has been well documented via a Smithsonian special available on Netflix, and for a few years, curious viewers could see a recreation of the behemoth as it travelled around the country. Half science, half circus, it attracted crowds at the Florida Museum of Natural History, the Las Vegas Natural History Museum, the Mississippi

Museum of Natural Science, and many other locations throughout the United States.

The discovery of an entirely new Paleocene species in Cerrejón, Colombia, must have been a coup for archeologists, the kind you wait your whole lifetime to discover. Cerrejón is a unique spot by any measure—it's known for hosting one of the largest coal operations in the world as well as being a treasure trove for fossils.[1] Around 58 million years ago (post-dinosaurs), the jungle boasted an array of enormous creatures, but nothing was as fearsome as Titanoboa. In *Smithsonian Magazine*, Guy Gugliotta helps us visualize by mentioning that the snake's width would come up to about a man's waist. The size alone is enough to grab hold of your imagination in the same way that the anaconda did when I was a child. When bored, I would often flip through our *Encyclopedia Britannica* set, dwelling mostly in the animal sections, though the human internal systems with their transparent overlays were a curiosity, too. I would pick out my favorite breed of dog, then favorite breed of cat. But I'd also look at the various snakes, and the anaconda seemed as real to me as a Pegasus or a fairy. Its sheer girth made it unbelievable until I saw one in person at the Tennessee Aquarium. Behind glass, the animal didn't seem quite as intimidating.

There is a notion that we are attracted to what scares us, pulled and repelled simultaneously, that adrenaline is its own kind of drug. Headlines proclaim the world's tallest roller coaster—or fastest or twistiest—and horror movies dare us not to scream. Sarah Perry's gothic historical novel *The Essex Serpent* features an enormous water snake terrorizing the locals. Part of what's so frightening about this particular beastie is that it lurks; it can't be seen. And it's easy to be scared of what we can't see or don't understand. Also, it's a big snake. If you want to make something scary scarier, all you have to do is make it larger. Godzilla, King Kong, Mothra, Nancy in *Attack of the 50 Foot Woman*. While your typical adult male great white shark grows to around twelve feet, the one in *Jaws* was twenty-five. (Female great whites top out around twenty-one.) Giants, ogres, cyclopses. That flesh-hungry plant in *Little Shop of Horrors*. In Japanese folklore there's an uwabami, an overgrown boa constrictor that preys on peasants. And on Mt. Tsurugi you'll supposedly find a behemoth of a serpent guarding King Solomon's treasures. As recently as the 1970s, workers in the forest claimed to have seen the creature.[2]

An anaconda caused quite a stir in New Jersey's Lake Hopatcong when several alleged sightings caused residents to panic. Snakegate, *People Magazine* thoughtfully dubbed it, due to officials supposedly swearing a reptile specialist to secrecy about the snake's real identify. (Locals thought it was a boa constrictor—still scary, but not as uncommon in the region since they're often kept as pets and can be lost or released.) If you like your snake gossip, you'll be happy to hear that *Reptile Magazine* says the whole story was made up, a new urban legend. And I know what you're thinking: Did the snake have a Twitter account? Of course it did: @HopatcongBoa. But it never received the kind of following as the baby cobra that escaped from the Bronx Zoo, currently at 150,000 followers eight years after he hit the town to take in the sights. Other US lake monsters include the Eel Pig of Herrington Lake, the Giant Octopus of Lake Thunderbird, and the Honey Island Swamp Monster. Lake Chelan in Washington has a winged alligator-snake. A lot of your monster snakes have wings, making them a little more dragon than serpent.

In 2010, I went to the Museum of Modern Art (MoMA) in Manhattan to see an exhibition by artist Gabriel Orozco. When I lived in New York City, I sat in the sculpture garden or stared at the Monet waterlilies on a semi-regular basis, and I was lucky enough to see a lot of special shows. To be perfectly honest, though, the only one I really remember is the Orozco, specifically the whale. *Mobile Matrix* lived on the second floor in—if I recall correctly—a room of its own. Suspended from the vaulted ceiling, the whale skeleton filled the space and cast a huge shadow on the floor that you could interrupt by walking through it. You sensed your own insignificance. So small in comparison, so ordinary. The piece felt like an embodiment of the sublime. It created an emotional response in me of awe and—while not quite terror—at least the sensation of being overwhelmed.

In contrast, despite being a real, extinct animal, there's something over-the-top about the presentation of Titanoboa. The recreation isn't just a full-size display of the snake, serenely—or even menacingly—staring at visitors. No, it's a recreation in action, the prehistoric snake swallowing an alligator, an armor-plated tail disappearing down the beast's gullet. It's not a representation of the sublime so much as the grotesque. It's intended to instill fear or perhaps nausea. Depiction after depiction of the animal shows it devouring some poor creature. In one, it looms above a human, mouth agape. The poster for the documentary shows Titanoboa swimming toward the viewer, ready to strike with its rows of jagged teeth, overlaid in bold, all caps with TITANOBOA: MONSTER SNAKE. It has the air of a carnival poster, a barker's call to see the abomination behind the curtain. It sensationalizes a genuinely impressive archeological discovery, stirring up interest but also making the snake a novelty act rather than a piece of history. In some ways, the alligator-gobbling depiction is the opposite of Orozco's respectful whale whose bones were excavated from a beach with permission of the Mexican government and painstakingly preserved for the artwork. To be fair, with the Smithsonian exhibition, you could also see Titanoboa's skeleton, an impressive find by any measure. I say "skeleton," but actually twenty-eight of these bone sets have been discovered in Colombia so far.

On a recent trip to New York City, I stopped at a bodega for a sandwich then wandered into Prospect Park in search of a quiet spot to enjoy my lunch. For once since I started this adventure of a book, I wasn't thinking about snakes. They found me, of course, as they are wont to do. It's a bit like hearing a new word for the first time, then noticing it everywhere. Or a particular shade of pink that's suddenly on every T-shirt and in every storefront. I suppose our minds are attracted to patterns, and my mind's serpentine lately. (Not to be confused with reptilian, supposedly the oldest of our evolutionary brains, the one that concerns basic urges.) For whatever the reason, snakes found me, not as Emily Dickinson's "narrow Fellow in the Grass," but as decoration. Fourteen large urns line the Army Plaza entrance to the park, each one sporting four snakes that do—I'll admit—look a little foreboding. Their expressions are downright sinister. They're also impressive, cast iron replicas of the 1890s originals chosen by Stanford White. They're not Titanoboa big, but at least cobra-sized, though their actual species is indistinguishable. Just snakes and, even more remarkably, not part of any obvious mythology. It seems as if White liked them, and so do I. They look a little perturbed, as if they'd rather be left alone. Not a bad mascot for New Yorkers, now that I think about it.

Across the street at the Brooklyn Public Library, you'll find a golden serpent on one of the pylons, coiled and ready to strike though expressionless, in the Art Deco style created by sculpture C. Paul Jennewein. The animal guards Athena, most commonly known as goddess of wisdom but who is also goddess of the serpent. You want more snakes in the area? There was once a rumor of a giant, real one that lived in the park, but that story never gained as much momentum as the Lake Hopatcong anaconda.

Not for nothing, new living snake species are also being discovered, particularly in remote regions of the world. In 2006, two different Kapuas mud snakes were found that can change color as a defense mechanism, like chameleons.[3] Dr. Sara Ruane, a Rutgers professor and herpetologist who specializes in evolution, currently studies the diversity of New Guinea ground snakes. It can be so challenging to catch a single specimen during fieldwork that some published studies include "person hours per snake" as a statistic: the average amount of time spent looking for a particular species versus the number of those beauties actually found. Sometimes Ruane likes to calculate the value of the snakes she brings back from an expedition, factoring in all the time spent catching them, and draws a simple conclusion: "Snakes are not cheap." But she also confesses that she loves the thrill of catching them.

Ruane had an early interest in reptiles and remembers telling her fifth-grade teacher that she wanted to be a herpetologist. She also kept a kiddie pool of salamanders in her grandparents' backyard. Her grandmother used to take her on long walks and say, "Let's flip this rock over and see what's under it." And while they mostly found bugs or debris, the occasional snake would keep them going, pulling the slot machine lever again and again. "It only takes one snake," Ruane explains, "to make you try another three hundred times."

Several of the experts I spoke to for this book mentioned that their interest in reptiles started with dinosaurs. Dr. David Blackburn with the Florida Museum of Natural History realized in college that he could "ask questions about the past using living animals"—that is, our ecological history isn't so far removed from the present. It can be seen in the jawless mouth of a lamprey or the armor of a crocodile, the sting of a scorpion and the strike of a snake. Even your backyard cardinal has 150 million-year-old ancestors. While it's appropriate to feel small when considering our planet—we're all just dust motes of impact in the grand scheme of things—it's also astonishing that we get to be here at all.

9 THE HOBBYIST

Within a matter of seconds, the hawk-moth caterpillar can transform into what looks like a pit viper. The end result isn't a rough approximation but a startlingly realistic subterfuge, right down to the heat pits. Even in a close-up video taken by filmmaker Filipe DeAndrade for the *National Geographic Wilds Untamed* series, the insect could be mistaken for a snake.[1] DeAndrade recalls jumping back as the hawk-moth tried to "strike" him. It's not unheard of for prey animals to pretend to be predators. There's even a term for it: defensive mimicry. A mimic octopus can present itself as an impressive fifteen different sea creatures.[2] The atlas moth boasts not one but two cobra heads on its wings. Perhaps unsurprisingly, pretending to be a snake seems to be the most common con in the animal kingdom. Plants are a whole other bag of masks.

In "Thoreau's Hound: Poetry and the Hidden," Jane Hirshfield mentions caterpillars traveling in a single head-to-toe line to resemble a serpent. The point, she maintains, is to hide in plain sight. In her essay, Hirshfield uses examples from nature to examine the purpose of art. "The real pleasure," she writes, "in murder mysteries, detective stories, comedies, tragedies of error, and poems—is found in grappling with an existence that has not been made simple."[3] Thus, she reimagines negative capability for a modern audience. When he coined the term "negative capability" in 1817, Keats was grappling with the notion of genius, specifically what qualities Shakespeare had that so many others lacked, and he alighted on the idea that a genius is someone comfortable with the unknown. Despite only mentioning the concept once in a letter, it caught on among poets that it's okay—preferable even—to start with questions rather than answers. A humbling of sorts. Or, as Ada Limón explains, "the poet, being most authentic and most attuned and connected to the universe, is not interested in the ego."[4] That's a beautiful philosophy, and one I fully endorse. How can we hope to surprise ourselves—or our readers—if we think we know everything already?

Poems themselves look a bit serpentine (prose poems notwithstanding). The lines wind down the page, gracefully and purposefully. They curve and curl. In her poem "Snake-Light," Natalie Diaz writes that "[t]he rattlesnake moves like sepia ink" and earlier refers to it as "[a] sentence, or a spell, a taut rope of emotion."[5] When touching a snakeskin, the speaker compares the motion to "the way I touch a line while reading." At times the animal represents language, at other times power, desire, family, violence. It is changeable but always important, always significant.

Caroline Seitz, the owner of Reptiles Alive LLC—an educational organization that brings animal shows to schools, town squares, and other events in Virginia, Maryland, and DC—gave her first presentation in fourth grade at the Hidden Oaks Nature Center, for which she borrowed a neighbor's boa constrictor because she only had a pet garter snake herself. Seitz's passion for snakes was clear in our conversation, and I couldn't help but be reminded of wildlife enthusiast Steve Irwin who challenged a lot of misconceptions about dangerous creatures with his various television appearances and shows. Seitz mentioned Irwin as well, specifically her naivety in thinking that organizations like hers would soon be unnecessary given his popularity. She thought the world would be a kinder place for animals. While Irwin did seem to spark a sort of sea change before his untimely death, we as a society—at least here in the United States—quickly slid backwards. Seitz discussed the suspicion of science she sees in the news and encounters in real life, a disheartening trend that can only have dire results. She summed it up memorably: "Irrational fear justifies a lot of cruelty."

While perhaps the most famous wildlife educator, Irwin was not the first and certainly won't be the last. There's a rich tradition of nature experts creating safe encounters for people in hopes of changing their minds. A lot of people in the US have never seen a snake in person— at least not outside of a zoo. How can we hope to appreciate that which we've never known? Not for research but for fun, I've watched more late-night television segments of Jack Hanna, Jeff Musial, and Robert Irwin (Steve Irwin's son) than I can recall. While always a little too rushed, this genre of interview delights me. I've watched Hanna present a striped hyena to David Letterman and Irwin pet bear cubs with Jimmy Fallon. Tarantulas, fennecs, and camels. Cheetahs, owls, and anteaters. Albino pythons that require guests—or band members from The Roots—to help out seem to be a crowd favorite. Comedian Will Ferrell even got in on the action once, bringing a short-spined Peruvian mongoose (a kitten), a Mongolian bush tiger (a guinea pig), a duck-bodied platypus (a duck), an upper Nile skull badger (a chipmunk), and a chicken to Stephen Colbert. While Ferrell is of course joking, the other conservationists are serious about their missions, however lighthearted their presentations. They've got seven minutes to convince a skeptical viewer at home that an alligator or a Gila monster is beautiful or—perhaps even better—cute. In general, we don't like to harm things that are cute.

Seitz noted that how poorly we treat animals is often linked to prizing sensationalism over science. In the Florida Everglades, invasive plants and insects do as much damage to the ecosystem as pythons, but pythons sell newspapers. And not only is it legal to hunt them, any means of execution is acceptable, despite the fact that snakes feel pain just like cats and dogs. "People truly believe that snakes are evil," Seitz says, and it's hard to argue with her reasoning.

Religion—like poetry and art and philosophy and science—gives us a way to explore the unknown, to push on the limits of our understanding and wrestle with our own mortality. The problem, as always, is human misuse. And we can see the catastrophic results of misconstruing that man has "dominion over the fishes of the sea, and the fowls of the air, and the beasts, and the whole earth, and every creeping creature that moveth upon the earth."[6] As icebergs collapse into the Arctic Ocean and fires rage in California, as droughts devastate agriculture in Iran and hurricanes wipe out large swaths of the Caribbean, we can see the results of abusing our planet, of taking our superiority for granted. Scientists are often accused of being elitist, but what could be farther from reality? Scientists must be, more than anything, humble. They must not only be aware of what they don't know, but excited about that ignorance. They want to shine light on what is presently dark.

Keats defined negative capability as a willingness to dwell "in uncertainties, Mysteries, doubts, without any irritable reaching after fact and reason."[7] It's no easy task, being comfortable with the unknown, with the unknowable. Admitting that you do not understand something takes a swallowing of pride, but letting go of the need to be an expert on everything—or rather, appearing to be an expert on everything—is freeing, as well. It's where genuine progress is made. To advance, to move forward, we must acknowledge that there is somewhere to go, that we have not reached our destination.

In his book *Rebuilding an Enlightened World: Folklorizing America*, folklorist Dr. Bill Ivey explores this question: How did we arrive here, at a society increasingly hostile to human rights, reason, and science?[8] He posits that American identity is local, that stories—not politics—are how we understand each other. This view offers much needed insight into why so many are willing to believe damning and entirely contrived conspiracy theories presented by websites pretending to be trustworthy organizations. It's the same impulse that makes people insist that Elvis is still alive and that Bigfoot wanders around forests in the Pacific Northwest. If a friend of a friend claims a story is true, there's no easy way to check for accuracy but also not much of an impulse to object, especially if the story reinforces our existing beliefs.

Narrative, as novelists well know, moves us more than data.

While I marvel at people who have always found snakes to be captivating, I don't count myself among their lot. I distinctly remember running from a mall pet store in Nashville because a well-meaning employee wanted to show off a boa constrictor he was holding. I've screamed at a crafts fair mistaking a stick for a slitherer. I've screamed at the Delaware Water Gap encountering a ribbon snake sunning itself an inch from my hand. On a school wilderness walk, at the Coney Island amusement park, when one fell from a tree into a family member's canoe. What I mean to say is that I get it. And yet, the more reptile facilities I've visited and festivals I've attended, the more photos I've browsed online, the more I've become fascinated rather than afraid. What else don't I know? I want to be surprised.

The snake identification group I joined on Facebook has strict rules. No discussion allowed, only identification and a note on whether the animal is venomous or nonvenomous. No guessing, and two wrong answers will get you banned. No angry or sad emoji reactions, although a simple "like" seems to be okay. Occasionally a member will sneak in a question before administrators disable comments, and a common one relates to the note on venom. A lot of curious people believe—as I once did—that there are established ways to spot a venomous snake, including triangular heads and vertical, slit pupils. But cobras as well as mambas and boomslangs have round pupils, and perfectly safe snakes can flatten their heads into arrows.

Like the hawk-moth, humans employ their own defense mechanisms. Runners wear reflective clothing at night, and kids about to be bullied might crack a joke. Some women, including me, use a sort of half smile when responding to street harassment to avoid escalation. For The Cut, novelist R. O. Kwon writes about why she wears dark, heavy eyeliner as a way to deflect assumptions about her personality, including racist stereotypes: "With my makeup, my shoes, my language, and my hands, every day I'm out in the world, I'm trying to offset what I fear you'll think of me."[9] Then there are our internal impulses to repress, project, and deny. We are, in our own ways, masters of disguise. That often means hiding what makes us vulnerable. But admitting what we don't know shouldn't be considered a vulnerability as much as an asset. How boring would life be if we knew everything already, had read every book and listened to every song? Had seen every animal? It must be possible to resist simplicity in favor of complexity, however befuddled and imperfect.

10 SHARPER THAN A SERPENT'S TOOTH

What does it mean to be afraid? Physical signs include dilated pupils, shortness of breath, sweaty palms. But it's what can't be seen—the internal roiling—that makes the sensation so awful. Fear makes us sick. Not weak, of course, as Franklin D. Roosevelt assured us: "Courage is not the absence of fear, but rather the assessment that something else is more important than fear." And yet it can certainly feel like an obstacle, sometimes an insurmountable one. Like 7.6 percent of the general population, I suffer from something called sleep paralysis.[1] Occasionally I will wake up in the middle of the night unable to move or speak and filled with terror that someone is watching me, just out of sight. It's fairly common for people with anxiety disorders. The phenomenon is, believe it or not, the result of our bodies trying to help us. At some point during our sleep cycle, our muscles relax to the point of being useless. The intended result? To keep us from sleepwalking. Because the mind is so close to the dreaming state, sleep paralysis can also be accompanied by hallucinations. This has led to folklore explanations, often in the form of a demon sitting on a person's chest. In some cultures, there is a specific entity like Pisadeira in Brazil, and in others there are more general night hags or spirits. Perhaps there is comfort in being able to name our fears, to identify them.

As familiar as the Roosevelt speech is, the cliché "frozen in fear" remains more commonly used. Best embodied by the mythology of Medusa, being frozen in fear means being helpless, beyond hope. A single glance at the gorgon's face, ringed with writhing serpents, could turn a person to stone. Adam Fuss's photograph *Medusa* graced the brochure cover for *Phantom Bodies: The Human Aura in Art*, an exhibition at the Frist Art Museum in Nashville. It was the first artwork I remember encountering when I walked into the space. In this large, 8-by-5-foot image, a transparent, old-fashioned dress seems to float against a black background, revealing a nest of snakes curving and intersecting inside. Instead of serpents replacing her hair, this modern interpretation sees Medusa as embodied by snakes—her soul *is* snakes, an internal rather than an external curse.

Fuss has been called a spirit photographer, though he rejects the term.[2] He uses a cameraless technique, a DIY pinhole device that can be made by poking a hole in a cardboard box and placing film inside. The results are uncanny, art that seems to occupy a liminal space between our world and an unknowable one beyond. One of his most famous works is a single snake rippling through water. According to a 2015 article for Artsy, he keeps around twenty snakes in plastic containers, each labeled with personalities such as "Nice-ish" and "Biter!! Mean."[3] The piece was published in conjunction with a show at Cheim and Reid called λόγος, a Greek term that does not have an easy translation into English but comes from "λέγω," or "I say," and denotes a connection between the divine and the earthly. And Fuss is clear that he thinks snakes get a bad rap. In an interview with Andrea Blanch, he points to the inherent contradiction in how we as a society view this animal, highlighting negative and positive portrayals. He mentions Medusa as well as ambulances. "The snake represents a lot of things, but one of them is that it carries the energy that manifests sexual attraction. It carries the energy of the future of the race."[4]

It's a lot of weight to put on one creature, a symbol of both life and death. And Fuss is certainly not the only artist to explore this contradiction. In Giovanni Bellini's *Four Allegories: Falsehood (Wisdom)* (1490), a man emerges from a shell, a snake wrapped around his outstretched arms. As can be seen from the title, there's an inherent conflict. Is the snake offering the figure lies or truth? The animal's and man's mouths are open as if in dialogue. This painting is part of a set, two representing virtues and two vices, but as art historian Dr. Rona Goffen points out in her text *Giovanni Bellini*, these panels have caused quite a bit of uncertainty. She posits "[p]erhaps these panels have caused scholars so much iconographic confusion precisely because they were Bellini's personal fantasy, not a compilation of more readily recognizable symbols imposed by a patron."[5]

At the Musée des Beaux-Arts in Paris, you'll find Paulus Bor's *Allegory of Syllogism* (1630–35). A woman holds a small, seemingly harmless snake, in this case a representation of deductive reasoning, of sound logic. It's almost a reimagining of Eve, not as the cause of humankind's downfall but as a source of wisdom. In Domenichino's 1626 *The Rebuke of Adam and Eve*, Eve can be seen somewhat comically (if you have a gallows sense of humor) pointing accusingly at a serpent that slithers away into the trees; Adam seems to be shrugging as if to say, "What could I do? She's very pretty." There's John Collier's overtly sexual 1887 *Lilith* (Adam's first wife in Jewish folklore) in which a large python wraps a woman's naked body, coming to rest its head on her shoulder where she tenderly reciprocates, resting her cheek against its scales. Many depictions of the Garden of Eden suggest the basic duality of the tree representing both good and evil; the serpent must somehow navigate these two worlds as well.

The contrasting depictions of virtue and vice recall William Blake's *Songs of Innocence* (1789) and *Songs of Experience* (1794), and while he does not have a poem in these collections dedicated specifically to a serpent, reptilian imagery abounds in his work. In "Auguries of Innocence," for example, envy's sweat is described as poison from a snake or a newt. "The Little Lost Girl" is divided by an illustration of a vine turning into a snake right under the couplet "And the desert wild / Become a garden mild," the first indication in the poem that the child is not in any danger from the animals.[6] There's also Blake's *Elohim Creating Adam* (1795) in which we see a snake curled around the length of Adam's body, a suggestion of either his impending mortality or his birth.

Perhaps my favorite artistic snake rendering, because I can see it in person (along with Domenichino's *The Rebuke of Adam and Eve*) at the National Gallery DC where I now live, is Eugène Delacroix's *The Tiger and the Snake* (1862). In this vibrant painting, both creatures are decidedly fierce, facing off with their teeth exposed. You can imagine the growls and hisses in their encounter, captured in almost vibrating brush strokes. A casual glance on a particularly tired day might make it seem as if they were animated, come to life in order to fight to death.

If you are someone who shudders at the very mention of scales, allow me for a moment to try to convince you that snakes are beautiful. I won't start with the drab water snake of North America nor with the speckled rat snakes that populated my childhood. Let's start grand with the African bush viper that comes in a variety of vivid shades. One kind looks like nothing so much as a flame come to life, its vivid orange and yellow pattern jagged rather than smooth, bold and precise. (Like millions of others, I watched the Season 8 premier of *Game of Thrones*, and the dragons seem modeled after bush vipers, right down to their bright yellow irises and slit pupils.) If living fire isn't your bag, they will sometimes change their hue: Perhaps a more oceanic blue would begrudgingly nudge you toward appreciation, skin that could be waves seen from a low-flying airplane. But if venom prevents you from admiration—and bush vipers are certainly venomous—I offer the San Francisco garter snake. Clocking in around three feet, this species is really a looker, turquoise body with red and black pinstripes. Coincidence or not, every photo I've ever seen of this little one looks like it's smiling, appropriately confident. And what about the sunbeam, which resembles, well, a sunbeam? This friend can be found in Southeast Asia and Indonesia showing off its iridescence to anyone fortunate enough to spot one. And if their movement scares you, what could be more graceful than that serpentine curve? They glide on land! It's no wonder that poets like D. H. Lawrence fancied them:

> For he seemed to me like a king,
> Like a king in exile, uncrowned in the underworld
> And so, I missed my chance with one of the lords
> Of life.[7]

In four short lines, Lawrence implies that life and death (the underworld) coexist in one limbless animal. Impressive.

In Zora Neale Hurston's famous short story "Sweat," an abusive husband decides to scare his wife by bringing home a six-foot rattlesnake and keeping it in a box by the front porch. It becomes the talk of the town, naturally. Like a shotgun appearing in the first act, we know what's going to happen with the snake. When Delia returns from a church service one night, she speaks to it, calling it old Satan and wondering why it's not stirring as usual. The box is quiet because the rattlesnake is no longer inside. Instead, her husband Sykes has put the snake in her laundry basket. When Delia finds it, she's terrified, but Hurston seems to appreciate the animal and writes that he was "pouring his awful beauty from the basket upon the bed."[8] Delia flees the house and hides. When her husband returns, he encounters the rattlesnake, which bites and kills him, Delia unable—or unwilling—to help. And now the 10th-grade essay question: What does the snake symbolize? Is it death for Sykes or life for Delia? Is it awful, or is it beautiful?

While our fear of snakes seems to be straightforwardly biological, artistic representations of this creature often complicate this dynamic. There's an ambiguity that challenges what T. S. Eliot would call the "objective correlative," his theory that some things have collective rather than individual meaning—that is, a rainbow after a storm implies hope to most people. Yet what could be more symbolic than a snake? As Fuss mentions, we see it on ambulances and hospitals, offering comfort to patients in search of healing. We see it on the Gadsden flag, warning instigators to leave well enough alone. There's the snake eating its own tail and the snake shedding its skin. It saves and kills, dies and is reborn. The cover of Michiko Kakutani's book *The Death of Truth: Notes on Falsehood in the Age of Trump* features a snake writhing up out of a speech bubble. But does the animal represent the truth or the falsehood of the title?

You don't have to search too hard for artistic depictions. We've got a wide range of Cleopatras, Medusas, and Eves. There's the famous *Laocoön and*

His Sons sculpture, excavated in Rome and currently on display at the Vatican, in which a priest struggles to protect his children from two enormous serpents. There's also El Greco's muscular, seventeenth-century interpretation of the same story in which the father grips one of the snakes by its neck before it strikes his face. While the animals here are not quite as ambiguous as in other depictions—they're clearly the cause of great suffering—the moral of the story is still up for debate. It's unclear whether Laocoön is being punished for trying to save the Trojans from the infamous horse ruse or for breaking his vow of celibacy.

I slept overnight in a cave once, and I don't think I'd like to repeat the experience. Absolute darkness, the kind where you truly cannot see your hand—or someone else's—in front of your face evoked panic rather than calm. I did not suddenly find myself in a state of peaceful meditation but rather having a sort of twelve-year-old's version of an existential crisis. What if death is a state of moving around in the dark forever—or worse, being frozen there? It was a Girl Scout camping trip, not a child-wanders-into-trouble sort of event, but I'd be hard-pressed to call it fun. It wasn't traumatic, though, and to be honest, I'd forgotten about this foray into spelunking until I read about archeologists finding cave drawings in the Cumberland Plateau: I may have slept near artwork hundreds of years old and as an adult writing in a well-lit room next to my softly snoring dog, that strikes me as remarkable.

The Native American drawings are in hard-to-reach places. The artists crawled deep, sometimes miles, into the caves. The Mud Glyph images are around eight hundred years old, made with charcoal, but other Southeastern cave discoveries date back to 4000 BC.[9] These are ancient works of art—spiders, birds, and serpents with horns, the kinds of depictions that can also be seen in Zuni pottery of the Southwest from a similar time period. At the Smithsonian National Museum of Natural History, pots on display show a host of animals, including skinny snakes with disproportionately large heads, mouths agape. Not fierce, but lively, as if moving up the sides.

Perhaps it is the snake's strangeness, its unique appearance and movement, that makes us eager to assign it meaning. We want to make sense of what we don't understand. By that logic, the snake is the most poetic of creatures, the embodiment of Keats's negative capability. (Not for nothing, Keats has a long poem, "Lamia," about a woman who was turned into a serpent.) Are we capable of regarding the serpent with wonder? Is it possible to reclaim the snake as an animal and not a sign, a living part of nature, not an object for our storytelling benefit? That doesn't seem likely anytime soon given the popularity of snakes as stand-ins for evil in pop culture. Nagini in *Harry Potter*, Sir Hiss in the animated *Robin Hood*, Mara in *Doctor Who*, a whole bunch in *Snakes on a Plane*. But maybe we can challenge our perceptions, recognize the grace alongside the fangs and venom. Complicated. Sublime. Awful and beautiful together.

11 MAGNANIMITY AND TRUE COURAGE

Britain has only one venomous snake, a bright-eyed fellow called the adder. And because of warmer temperatures, he's now active year-round.[1] That's a big change for an animal accustomed to hibernating from fall to early spring. Their increased numbers don't mean that they're thriving, though. In fact, the adder is currently at risk of becoming extinct in the United Kingdom, mostly because of humans killing them. Or, as naturalist and television host Iolo Williams explains, the adder has an image problem. It strikes fear in residents, though nobody's died from a bite in more than four decades. Williams warns that "we can do survey work and try and protect them, but my strong feeling is that if we don't change how people feel about them, show they're not dangerous and are something to look after then we will lose them."[2]

According to Endangered Species International, there are currently 203 reptiles listed as Vulnerable, 134 as Endangered, and another 86 as Critically Endangered.[3] And if you're wondering why we should care, the loss of even a single species can affect our sensitive ecosystems. While people killing them is only part of the problem (loss of habitat also plays a key role), it's worth considering the consequences of our own ophidiophobia, even our apathy; apathy about the environment in general has gotten us into a whole heap of trouble. As temperatures rise and glaciers crash into the sea, we're already seeing an increase in floods, heat waves, hurricanes, and other natural disasters (tripling since the 1960s). To be honest, the loss of a few danger noodles doesn't seem that bad in comparison. But consider the good that can come from leaving them be.

If you've never killed a snake yourself, you probably know someone who has. It's a common enough practice in rural communities, even though snakes keep down rodent populations, preventing the spread of diseases and protecting crops. A few years ago, the owner of a dog-boarding facility in Florida learned this lesson the hard way. When he found snakes living in his kennel rafters, he got rid of them all only to be invaded by rats. The vermin damaged the facility's structure, feasted on the dog food, and generally made an expensive nuisance of themselves for two years until the situation could be controlled again.[4] All of which is to say, nature has a better handle on its business than humans do, but that doesn't stop us from meddling.

In their study on the causes and consequences of extinction, Navjot S. Sodhi, Barry W. Brook, and Corey J. A. Bradshaw conclude that "[a]lthough extinctions are a normal part of evolution, human modifications to the planet in the last few centuries, and perhaps even millennia, have greatly accelerated the rate at which extinctions occur. Habitat loss remains the main driver of extinctions, but it may act synergistically with other drivers such as overharvesting and pollution, and, in the future, climate change." They also note that loss of pollinators can have dire consequences, including the collapse of entire ecosystems.[5]

Like birds, reptiles can also redistribute seed and are a food source themselves. If that doesn't turn your head, there are plenty of nonvenomous snakes that kill and eat the venomous ones. In North America, we have the indigos and the kingsnakes. In South America, there's the bona fide assassin the mussurana that dines on vipers. (The mussurana is technically venomous, but harmless to humans.) Snakes' potential for advancing life-saving drugs seems boundless. As Dr. Harvey B. Lillywhite explains in his important book *How Snakes Work*, "The efficacy of venoms and the diversity of their pharmacological properties have fascinated humans since the time of Aristotle, and the ancients developed many snake products—including blood, venom, and viscera—that were used in various medical remedies of the time."[6] He goes on to extol the value of venom in treatment advances for everything from cancer to muscular dystrophy. Cobra venom was even instrumental in the discovery of DNA. Snakes' locomotion is also currently being studied by Georgia Tech physicists to help improve robotics for search-and-rescue missions and—perhaps in the future—distant planet exploration.[7]

The Complex Rheology and Biomechanics (CRAB) lab at Georgia Tech led by Dr. Daniel Goldman combines the seemingly disparate fields of robotics, physics, and biology. It studies how animals move in complex environments and has worked with a range of animals, from fire ants to salamanders. The snake experiments have received the most media attention, though, including the lab's work with sidewinder rattlesnakes. This particular pursuit included a partnership with Zoo Atlanta where the snakes were kept. (No venomous species are kept on the Georgia Tech campus for any worried parents out there.) Sidewinders are unique because of the technique they've developed for navigating sandy terrain, a movement that at first looks counterintuitive: The animal throws its mid-section forward, what might be ineloquently called "scooting." The sidewinder can quickly traverse shifting landscapes, reaching speeds of up to eighteen miles per hour.

While the venomous nature of the study might raise a few eyebrows, studying nature to improve human technologies is nothing new. Perhaps most famously, Velcro came from observing the way burrs stick to dogs' fur. The US Navy is currently funding studies that focus on the unique capabilities of shark skin with hopes of creating faster ships.[8] And the wonder of spider webs might lead to better wound care. We've learned from bird beaks, bat sonar, and even plant hibernation.

Dr. Jennifer Rieser is a postdoc at Georgia Tech's CRAB lab who focuses on snake scattering. She hopes to improve robots' ability to deal with obstacles in their paths by observing how snakes handle similar encounters, specifically how the Western shovel-nosed snake navigates its surroundings. The team discovered that the snakes do not consciously avoid objects; instead, when their bodies touch a surface, they move accordingly. In that way, they resemble light waves, and Goldman calls this "the most beautiful phenomena" they've discovered. I'll add that the shovel-nosed is pretty on its own, even without its unique movement. It's a small species, growing to about a foot in length. Its pattern is striking with bands of black and sometimes orange against a light background. Tigers could have gotten their inspiration from this little guy.

Goldman explains that the origins of these experiments were serendipitous. He was in the desert with a team of herpetologists from Zoo Atlanta looking for sidewinders at night when a shovel-nosed crossed the road in front of them, moving with surprising speed over the surface. They decided to catch a few of them to study. The shovel-nosed is a sand swimmer—it immerses itself in sand and moves through it—but has also clearly adapted a way to move efficiently on the surface. The lab's work could lead to a new type of robot, one more adaptable and therefore more successful in a variety of operations.

Rieser talks about this work in animated tones, explaining complex ideas in an accessible manner. She offered the working hypothesis for why shovel-nosed do not deviate from their wave shape, mentioning what she called a "passive mechanical response": The snake's body reacts without having to communicate with its brain. When asked about whether she had any apprehensions about working with reptiles, Rieser said no, even though she wasn't the kind of kid who kept snakes in an aquarium. Even so, she speaks quite naturally about the wonder of this animal and its many interesting interactions. She mentions with appreciation how different types of snakes have developed different strategies for navigating granular terrains. It seems as if there is no limit to their ingenuity.

I spoke with Dr. Perrin Schiebel about the actual snakes used in these studies. She told me that the snakes, four to fifteen at a time, are housed in what she calls a "fancy snake hotel," Georgia Tech's Physiological Research Facility. While distinctions between species are more noticeable, even among the Western shovel-nosed there are differences in personality. Some are skittish while others more aggressive; a few are too docile, too malleable, to be of much use in the lab. Like people, some get tired after a while and stop cooperating. It's easy to think of snakes as unfeeling, and while there's no scientific way to measure their emotions, it seems like they have them. They are more individual than we might at first assume. On occasion, local snakes will find their way into the building's lobby, and Schiebel has been called to fetch them, her colleagues assuming that one of her test subjects escaped. While she would never be so careless, she also doesn't mind catching the lost critters and releasing them back into the wild. She doesn't recall ever being afraid of snakes. (Centipedes, on the other hand, are a whole other story.)

The snakes caught indoors do not move quickly, which relates to Schiebel's studies that compare how sand snakes move to how generalist snakes move. (Your backyard corn snake can maneuver over a wide variety of terrains as well as climb trees and even swim.) She is participating in a tradition that dates back centuries. Scientists have long been interested in animal locomotion, but new technologies and interdisciplinary collaborations have made it possible to dig deeper into the subject. "Even the simple model organism," Schiebel explains, "is complicated. There's so much we don't know." While their approaches might be different, there's definitely a kinship between scientists and artists exploring the unknown, reveling in questions as much as in answers. There's a particular type of confidence involved, a confidence grounded in uncertainty, that it's okay to begin at a place of curiosity.

In 2017, thirty-four reptiles died overnight at Zoo Knoxville under mysterious circumstances. My obsession with the story didn't last long because it proved difficult to get any updates. After "toxic substances" were determined to be the cause of death, there seemed to be an unacknowledged shrug from the public. Not even an unsolved case in a nation of true crime addicts could keep the story in our collective conversation. The source of the toxins was never discovered, but who's going to mourn the loss of a few vipers and skinks, never mind that several of the victims were endangered. Imagine if thirty-four big cats met a similar fate, or even thirty-four parrots. Twitter would certainly be aflutter.

What is it about snakes that makes many of us ambivalent about their fates, if not actively hostile? Filmmaker Brianna Paciorka interviewed a Zoo Knoxville herpetologist about the tragedy. "There were quite a few snakes in there that I really loved, and unfortunately they didn't make it," Clara Lemyre said. "It's really heartbreaking when I'm outside and hear visitors say things like, 'Oh, I'm glad all those snakes died.'"[9]

I've spent a lot of time at Zoo Knoxville. Despite not living nearby, I have a membership, and my mom works in the gift shop. I often visit the reptile house when I'm in town, even though half the terrariums are inaccessible or empty now. On my last trip, I watched a man replace the water for a red spitting cobra. The Zoo Knoxville handout on this species lets us know that "They aim for the eyes, and hardly ever miss." Not exactly an encouraging endorsement. The handler put on goggles and used a spray bottle to gently persuade the creature to face away. With his free hand, he used a grabber to remove the water dish, refill it, and replace it. I'd say the operation took less than sixty seconds, but I held my breath the entire time. I then watched him repeat the process, goggle-less, for the critically endangered Aruba island rattlesnake. Zoo Knoxville estimates that there are fewer than 250 of these in the wild. In photos, this guy looks dusty—sand-colored—but in real life, he was almost peach. Zoo

Knoxville recently broke ground on an $18-million-dollar facility for reptiles and amphibians with a goal of expanding their conservation efforts.[10] They're betting on public interest in these species, that fear or fascination (or both) will bring people through the doors. Once there, they'll learn about these creatures while they shiver or smile.

There are a startling number of myths and misconceptions about snakes, beyond the greatest one: they are evil. There's Saint Patrick marching all the snakes from Ireland. They can dislocate their jaws in order to eat large prey. You can tell the age of a rattler by the rings on its tail. Snakes remember people who have harmed them or their mates. (Not true for snakes, but I recommend staying on the good side of crows.) They are attracted to bowls of milk, and perhaps my favorite, some of them can fly. To be fair, there are indeed gliding snakes. The paradise tree snake can jump and land a good distance away, even changing its direction as needed in the air. Naturalist Mike Davis shared with me a folklore quiz that he uses during his presentations. True or false: A dead snake on a fence means rain's coming.

It's difficult to change people's opinions. They'll seek out information that confirms their bias, unconsciously or not. We see evidence of this daily in social media posts and article comments. Information that might open someone's eyes is met with a response of "fake news." A few years ago, someone told me that there are no such things as facts. The example he used: If I say it's raining, and he says it's not, there's no way to know for sure. I'll admit the statement flummoxed me. How do you build on such a shaky foundation, a sandy terrain? If we can't agree on the weather, what can we agree on? I started asking friends about moments in their lives when they'd changed their minds about a topic. Several mentioned that becoming parents had altered their views. Kids shifted their priorities, what they thought was most important in life. And perhaps unsurprisingly, the future of the planet became a source of near-constant concern. How do we make sure there's an inhabitable planet for the next generation and the one after that? Changing perceptions of snakes might not seem related, but finding value in nature, including the parts we don't like, can help us make better choices. To put it another way: We don't want to be the dog kennel owner invaded by rats.

Scientists are unclear on how climate change will ultimately affect reptiles. The heartiest creatures, the cockroaches for example, will probably thrive in any future, however inhospitable. Those microorganisms making their cozy, little homes in volcanoes? They'll most likely be fine. But there are too many factors to make concrete predictions about the future of native snakes. Even those quickly populating non-native Florida pythons might find their food sources diminished. Some scientists believe that a mass extinction event is imminent, perhaps even already underway.[11] It's been about 65 million years since the last one.

Do animals experience wonder? Or is that a human privilege? A field lighting up unexpectedly with fireflies, a sunset making the sky turn impossibly pink. An ocean crashing into rocky cliffs or desert sands undulating in the heat. I'm partial to a sudden summer storm, rain blowing sideways and thunder rumbling in the distance. I like to feel insignificant for a few minutes, in awe of the power of nature. Then there's the way my dog, in a few short months, has learned to steer our walk toward the tree where pedestrians sometimes toss their leftover chicken bones. The way I will stick my hand in her mouth to remove them, not at all afraid of her sharp, wolfy teeth. And speaking of teeth, did you know that if you peer into the mouth of a viper (not recommended), you'll see extra fangs? Snake teeth replace themselves throughout the animal's life.

Curiosity, a state of interest, yes, but also of oddity. "That's curious," we might say as a mild exclamation of disbelief. It may be an easier goal than wonder, to remain open to learning something new, to like something not despite of its weirdness but because of it. Sure, there are other limbless creatures, but the snake is the one that we need for our mythologies, for our bedtime stories and scary movies. It is, of course, humans who do the most damage. In 2017, more than 17,000 people were murdered in the United States.[12] The CDC estimates that about five people die each year in this country from snakebites.[13] Moreover, the majority of people envenomated are bitten while trying to kill snakes that are simply defending themselves. These critters need an image makeover, a PR campaign that extols their values. They need, as it were, a good publicist.

In 1775, Benjamin Franklin wrote about why he believed the rattlesnake to be the perfect emblem of the colonies: "I recollected that her eye excelled in brightness, that of any other animal, and that she has no eye-lids—She may therefore be esteemed an emblem of vigilance.—She never begins an attack, nor, when once engaged, ever surrenders: She is therefore an emblem of magnanimity and true courage."[14] If we must make the snake into a symbol, an object, let us take our cue from the man who invented bifocals to help us see more clearly. Snakes are not our enemy, but we are theirs. And wouldn't it be better to have them on our side? A mascot rather than an omen of impending doom? It only takes a push in the right direction, a glint off the iridescent scales of a rainbow snake, a photo of a python in a birthday hat. How marvelous, we might say. How unexpected. And in that moment, we open up to possibilities, to a way of seeing the world beyond our assumptions. To curiosity, to wonder, to magnanimous and courageous creatures. To being better animals ourselves.

ACKNOWLEDGMENTS

I t is a privilege to have a book in the Object Lessons series. Thank you to Haaris Naqvi, Ian Bogost, and Christopher Schaberg for creating such a unique, compelling catalogue. I am particularly grateful to Chris for his editorial guidance. I am also grateful to be represented by the Ann Rittenberg Literary Agency. What an honor to work with Ann and her incredible team, including Rosie Jonker.

I've been amazed by the positive reactions to this project and would like to particularly acknowledge Kristen Linton, Katie Meadows, Ricardo Maldonado, Matthew Pennock, Toral Doshi, Tayt Harlin, Emily Mitchell, Eric Hupe, and Davin Rosborough. Thank you to David Burr Gerrard for telling me about *Holy Ghost People*, directed by his grandfather Peter Adair. An early version of the chapter "Kingsnakes and Beauty Queens" appeared in *Chapter 16*, expertly edited by Margaret Renkl. My parents Paula and Kevin Wright are my biggest fans, and none of this would be possible without them. My husband Adam Province is probably happy that I will no longer be sharing (so many) rattlesnake anecdotes with him. Nonetheless, his support means the world to me.

Snakes are more fascinating and important than my little book can convey. I am indebted to the conservationists, herpetologists, and enthusiasts who shared their knowledge with me. All mistakes are mine. There are many wonderful organizations that exist to educate the public about reptiles in general, save endangered species, and keep their human neighbors safe. Thank you to all of the people at places like Herpetological Conservation International, Wildlife SOS, and The Orianne Society who work tirelessly to create a better world for all creatures.

NOTES

Preface

1 Geoffrey Brewer, "Snakes Top List of Americans' Fears," Gallup, March 19, 2001, https://news.gallup.com/poll/1891/snakes-top-list-americans-fears.aspx.

Chapter 1

1 Jim Spellman, "Pageant hopefuls decapitate, skin snakes at Rattlesnake Roundup," CNN, March 12, 2011, http://www.cnn.com/2011/US/03/12/rattlesnake.roundup/index.html.

2 Sarah Gibbens, "Babies Confirm: Fear of Snakes and Spiders Is Hard-Wired," *National Geographic*, October 26, 2017.

3 *American Masters*, "Richard Avedon: Darkness and Light," directed by Helen Whitney, PBS, January 1996.

4 The Local, "IN PICTURES: Italy's annual snake festival," May 2, 2018, https://www.thelocal.it/20180502/pictures-italy-snake-festival-cocullo.

5 Ian Austen, "This Canadian Town Comes Alive Once a Year, as Thousands of Snakes Mate," *The New York Times*, June 16, 2019, https://www.nytimes.com/2019/06/16/world/canada/manitoba-narcisse-snakes.html.

Chapter 2

1 Department of Wildlife Ecology & Conservation, University of Florida, "Frequently Asked Questions About Venomous Snakes," accessed June 26, 2019, http://ufwildlife.ifas.ufl.edu/venomous_snake_faqs.shtml.

2 Eleonor Cummins, "We created a frankenhouse of the most common phobias," *Popular Science*, October 31, 2018, https://www.popsci.com/most-common-phobias/.

3 Sarah Gibbens, "Babies Confirm: Fear of Snakes and Spiders Is Hard-Wired," *National Geographic*, October 26, 2017.

4 Craig Hlavaty, "72-year-old woman kills 11 copperhead snakes in Oklahoma," *Houston Chronicle*, January 9, 2018.

5 John Milton, *Paradise Lost: A Poem in Twelve Books*, ed. Merritt Y. Hughes (Indianapolis, IN: Hackett, 2003), 16.

6 Sarah R. Morrison, "The Accommodating Serpent and God's Grace in 'Paradise Lost,'" *Studies in English Literature, 1500–1900* 49, no. 1 (2009): 173–95, http://www.jstor.org.ezproxy.snhu.edu/stable/40071390.

7 The National Institute for Occupational Safety and Health, Centers for Disease Control and Prevention, "Venomous Snakes," accessed June 26, 2019, https://www.cdc.gov/niosh/topics/snakes/default.html.

8 Lucille Clifton, "brothers" from *The Book of Light* (Port Townsend, WA: Copper Canyon Press, 1993), 69–76.

Chapter 3

1 Corey Flintoff, "In India, Snake Charmers Are Losing Their Sway," NPR, August 8, 2011, https://www.npr.org/2011/08/08/139086119/in-india-snake-charmers-are-losing-their-sway.

2 A. J. Racy, "Domesticating Otherness: The Snake Charmer in American Popular Culture," *Ethnomusicology* 60, 2 (2016): 197–232, doi: 10.5406/ethnomusicology.60.2.0197.

3 Karen Middleton, *Ancestors, Power, and History in Madagascar* (Leiden, Netherlands: Brill, 1999), 259.

4 Racy, "Domesticating Otherness," 197–232.

5 Evan Ross Katz, "Britney Spears is auctioning these iconic outfits from her music videos on eBay — and they're going for $100,000," Insider, May 10, 2017, https://www.insider.com/britney-spears-costumes-are-being-auctioned-on-ebay-2017-5.

6 MTV, "Britney Spears Shoots For Fun With Video Debut," December 18, 1999, https://web.archive.org/web/20100424051911/http://www.mtv.com/news/articles/1434423/19981218/spears_britney.jhtml.

7   Booth Moore, "They're first ladies of fashion too," *Los Angeles Times*, January 18, 2009, https://www.latimes.com/fashion/alltherage/la-ig-firstladies18-2009jan18-story.html.

Chapter 4

1   Anil Shetty, Shraddha Shetty, and Oliver Dsouza, "Medical Symbols: Myths vs Reality," *Journal of Clinical and Diagnostic Research* 8, no. 8 (2014): 12–14.

2   Lakshmi Gandhi, "A History of 'Snake Oil Salesman," NPR, Code Switch: Word Watch, August 23, 2013, https://www.npr.org/sections/codeswitch/2013/08/26/215761377/a-history-of-snake-oil-salesmen.

3   Britt Collins, "Poison Pass: The Man Who Became Immune to Snake Venom," *The Guardian*, February 11, 2018, https://www.theguardian.com/environment/2018/feb/11/poison-pass-the-man-who-became-immune-to-snake-venom-steve-ludwin.

4   Natural History Museum, "The Man Who Injects Himself with Venom," directed by Bucy McDonald, May 24, 2018, https://www.nhm.ac.uk/discover/the-man-who-injects-himself-with-venom.html.

5   BBC, "Meet the Man Who Injects Himself with Snake Venom," November 6, 2017, https://www.bbc.co.uk/programmes/p05m541d.

6   Douglas Martin, "Bill Haast, A Man Charmed by Snakes, Dies at 100," *New York Times*, June 17, 2011, https://www.nytimes.com/2011/06/18/us/18haast.html.

7 Kathy Lohr, "Adventures of a Snake Milker: The Herd Has Fangs," NPR, April 9, 2010, https://www.npr.org/templates/story/story.php?storyId=125036229.

8 *Nature*, "Venomous Cures," PBS, October 31, 2008, http://www.pbs.org/wnet/nature/the-reptiles-snakes-venomous-cures/2913/.

Chapter 5

1 Associated Press, "Relatives to Get Orphans of Snakebite Victims," *Los Angeles Times*, February 13, 1999, https://www.latimes.com/archives/la-xpm-1999-feb-13-mn-7757-story.html.

2 Allen G. Breed, "Custody Fight for Snake Handlers' Orphans Pits Faith Against Safety," *Los Angeles Times*, December 13, 1998, https://www.latimes.com/archives/la-xpm-1998-dec-13-mn-53450-story.html.

3 *Holy Ghost People*, directed by Peter Adair (1967, Thistle Films), documentary.

4 *Man and Snake*, episode 1, "The Serpent Preachers: Talking to God Through Snakes," on Vice, https://video.vice.com/en_us/video/vice-the-serpent-preachers-snake-man-episode-1/5b6c51c1be4077095a5890fb.

5 Jordan Nelson, "Preacher Opens up About 'Taking Up Serpents,' a Display of Faith," *Register Herald*, June 3, 2019, https://www.register-herald.com/west_virginia/preacher-opens-up-about-taking-up-serpents-a-display-of/article_b8794306-8fb4-538f-82ae-8400110e3478.html.

6 Mark 16:17-18 (NIV).

7 Leviticus 18:22 (NIV).

8 Matthew 10:16 (NIV).

9 Corinthians 13:13 (NIV).

10 Allen G. Breed, "Custody Fight for Snake Handlers' Orphans Pits Faith Against Safety," *Los Angeles Times*, December 13, 1998, https://www.latimes.com/archiv es/la-xpm-1998-dec-13-mn-53450-story.html.

Chapter 6

1 Ovid, *Metamorphoses*, trans. Charles Martin (New York: W. W. Norton, 2005), 155.

2 Sarah Bernice Wallace, "The Changing Faces of Medusa," *Reinvention: An International Journal of Undergraduate Research*, British Conference of Undergraduate Research (2011 Special Issue), accessed August 2, 2019, http://www.warwick.ac.uk/go/reinven tionjournal/archive/bcur2011specialissue/wallace.

3 Patricia Smith, *Big Towns, Big Talk* (Cambridge, MA: Zoland Books, 1992), 53.

4 Sarah Butler, "Gucci Owners Gets Teeth into Snakeskin Market with Python Market," *The Guardian*, January 25, 2017, https://www.theguardian.com/business/201 7/jan/25/gucci-snakeskin-python-farm-kering-saint-laurent-and-alexander-mcqueen.

5 Kering, "Kering, IUCN and ITC Form Partnership to Improve Python Trade," accessed August 2, 2018, https://www.kering.com/en/news/iucn-itc-form-partn ership-improve-python-trade.

6 Butler, "Gucci Owners," *The Guardian,* January 25, 2017, https://www.theguardian.com/business/2017/jan /25/gucci-snakeskin-python-farm-kering-saint-laure nt-and-alexander-mcqueen.

7 National Park Service, "Tanning in the Seventeenth Century," Lee Pelham Cotton, 1996, https://www.nps .gov/jame/learn/historyculture/tanning-in-the-seve nteenth-century.htm.

8 Ian Frazier, "SnakeLandia: Giant Pythons Invade the Everglades, Alarming Biologists and Hunters," *Smithsonian* 50, no 04 (2019): 66–81.

Chapter 7

1 Joshua Hammer, "On the Vodun Trail in Benin," *New York Times*, February 3, 2012.

2 Mary Oliver, *New and Selected Poems* (Boston: Beacon, 1992), 110.

3 Karen Brulliard, "Helping Solve the Wildest Crimes," *Washington Post*, August 30, 2018, https://www.was hingtonpost.com/news/national/wp/2018/08/30/featur e/when-the-crime-victim-is-an-animal-this-lab-is-o n-the-case/?utm_term=.7ea278759074.

4 US Fish & Wildlife Services, "The Reptile Black Market Is Still Around," accessed August 2, 2019, https://ww w.fws.gov/news/blog/index.cfm/2017/8/30/The-Reptil e-Black-Market-Still-Around.

5 Endangered Species International, "Ecological Roles of Reptiles," accessed August 3, 2019, https://www.end angeredspeciesinternational.org/reptiles3.html.

Chapter 8

1 Guy Gugliotta, "How Titanoboa, the 40-Foot-Long Snake, Was Found," *Smithsonian Magazine*, April 2012.

2 Brad Steiger, *Real Monsters, Gruesome Critters, and Beasts from the Darkside* (Detroit: Visible Ink Press, 2010), 103.

3 John Pickrell, "Chameleon Snake Can Turn White in Minutes," New Scientist, June 27, 2006, https://www.newscientist.com/article/dn9417-chameleon-snake-can-turn-white-in-minutes/.

Chapter 9

1 "This 'Snake' Is Really Just a Caterpillar with an Incredible Disguise," directed by Philipe DeAndrade, *National Geographic Wilds Untamed*, accessed August 5, 2019, https://video.nationalgeographic.com/video/untamed/00000162-300f-ddf6-a5eb-712f562a0000.

2 Courtney Ferrarese, "Defensive Mimicry: Wild Wizards of Trickery and Illusion," National Wildlife Federation (NWF), accessed August 5, 2019, https://blog.nwf.org/2016/02/defensive-mimicry-wild-wizards-of-trickery-and-illusions.

3 Jane Hirshfield, "Thoreau's Hound: Poetry and the Hidden," in *Ten Windows: How Great Poems Transform the World* (New York: Alfred A. Knopf, 2015), 107.

4 Diana Delgado, "Ada Limón: Connected to the Universe," *Guernica*, July 24, 2018, https://www.guernicamag.com/ada-limon-connected-to-the-universe/.

5   Natalie Diaz, *Postcolonial Love Poem* (Minneapolis: Graywolf Press, 2020), 83, 86.

6   Genesis 1:27 (NIV).

7   Poetry Foundation, "Negative Capability," accessed August 5, 2019, https://www.poetryfoundation.org/le arn/glossary-terms/negative-capability.

8   Bill Ivey, *Rebuilding an Enlightened World: Folklorizing America* (Bloomington: Indiana University Press, 2017).

9   R. O. Kwon, "Why I Don't Leave the House Without Putting on Black Eye Shadow," The Cut, April 6, 2018, https://www.thecut.com/2018/04/why-i-always-wear-b lack-eyeshadow.html.

Chapter 10

1   Esther Olunu et al., "Sleep Paralysis, a Medical Condition with a Diverse Cultural Interpretation," *International Journal of Applied and Basic Medical Research* vol. 8,3 (2018): 137–42, doi:10.4103/ijabmr. IJABMR_19_18.

2   Andrea Blanch, "Outlier: Interview with Adam Fuss," *Musée*, accessed August 6, 2019, http://museemagazine. com/features/35238.

3   Alexxa Gotthardt, "Adam Fuss on His Cameraless Images and Experimenting with Live Snakes," Artsy, September 21, 2015, https://www.artsy.net/article/art sy-editorial-adam-fuss-on-his-cameraless-images-and-experimenting.

4   Blanch, "Outlier: Interview with Adam Fuss," http://museemagazine.com/features/35238.

5   Rona Goffen, *Giovanni Bellini* (New Haven, CT: Yale University Press, 1989), 231.

6   William Blake, *The Complete Poetry and Prose of William Blake: With a New Foreword and Commentary by Harold Bloom* (Berkeley: University of California Press, 2008), 20.

7   D. H. Lawrence, *The Complete Poems of D. H. Lawrence* (Hertfordshire, UK: Wordsworth Editions, 1994), 284.

8   Zora Neale Hurston, *The Complete Stories* (New York: Harper Perennial, 1995), 83.

9   John Jeremiah Sullivan, "America's Ancient Cave Art," *The Paris Review* via *Slate*, March 20, 2011, https://slate.com/culture/2011/03/america-s-ancient-cave-art-mysterious-drawings-thousands-of-years-old-offer-a-glimpse-of-lost-native-american-cultures-and-traditions.html.

Chapter 11

1   Nicholas Milton, "Adders Now Active All Year with Warmer UK Weather," *The Guardian*, March 6, 2019, https://www.theguardian.com/environment/2019/mar/06/adders-now-active-all-year-with-warmer-uk-weather.

2   Steffan Messenger, "Adder Extinction Fear Over 'Image Problem' in the UK," BBC News, October 23, 2018, https://www.bbc.com/news/uk-wales-45942095.

3 Endangered Species International, "Endangered Reptiles," accessed August 8, 2019, https://www.bbc.com/news/uk-wales-45942095.

4 Nature, "Saving Snakes," PBS, October 31, 2008, https://www.pbs.org/wnet/nature/the-reptiles-snakes-saving-snakes/2911/.

5 Navjot S. Sodhi, Barry W. Brook, and Corey J. A. Bradshaw, "Causes and Consequences of Species Extinctions," in *The Princeton Guide to Ecology*, ed. Simon A. Levin (Princeton, NJ: Princeton University Press), 514–20.

6 Harvey B. Lillywhite, *How Snakes Work* (New York: Oxford University Press, 2014), 58–59.

7 Katherine J. Wu, "Let a Snake-Inspired Robot Be Your Hero Today," PBS, February 25, 2019, https://www.pbs.org/wgbh/nova/article/let-snake-inspired-robot-be-your-hero-today/.

8 Stephen Leahy, "Shark Skin Inspires Ship Coating," *Wired*, March 10, 2005, https://www.wired.com/2005/03/shark-skin-inspires-ship-coating/.

9 Amy McRary, "Unknown Toxin Killed 34 Zoo Knoxville Reptiles," *USA Today*, May 12, 2017, https://www.knoxnews.com/story/news/2017/05/12/unknown-toxin-killed-34-zoo-knoxville-reptiles/316341001/.

10 Maggie Jones, "Zoo Knoxville Announces New $18M, 2.5 acre Reptile, Amphibian Habitat," *Knoxville News Sentinel*, April 10, 2019, https://www.knoxnews.com/story/life/2019/04/10/zoo-knoxville-announces-new-18-m-reptile-amphibian-habitat/3414028002/.

11 Damian Carrington, "Earth's Sixth Mass Extinction Event Under Way, Scientists Warn," *The Guardian*, July 10, 2017, https://www.theguardian.com/environment/2017/jul/10/earths-sixth-mass-extinction-event-already-underway-scientists-warn.

12 FBI, "2017 Crime in the United States," accessed August 8, 2019, https://ucr.fbi.gov/crime-in-the-u.s/2017/crime-in-the-u.s.-2017/topic-pages/murder.

13 The National Institute for Occupational Safety and Health, Centers for Disease Control and Prevention, "Venomous Snakes," accessed June 26, 2019, https://www.cdc.gov/niosh/topics/snakes/default.html.

14 Benjamin Franklin, *A Benjamin Franklin Reader* (New York: Simon & Schuster, 2003), 264.

INDEX

"Accommodating Serpent, The, and God's Grace in *Paradise Lost*" (Morrison)   15–16

Adair, Peter   42, 44, 48

adders   97

Allegory of Syllogism (Bor)   88

American Masters series, PBS   4

anacondas   xiii, xv, 68, 69, 73

Angitia   5

antivenin   11, 33, 35, 37

Asclepius   6, 33

Assassination of Gianni Versace, The: American Crime Story, Netflix   57

Attack of the 50 Foot Woman (Juran)   69

Atwood, Margaret   24

Australia   26

Avedon, Richard   1, 2, 4, 25

"Baby One More Time" (Spears)   27

Bellini, Giovanni   87, 88

belly dancing   21, 23

Bible   45, 46, 48

Blackburn, David   74

black market   61

Blake, William   89

Blanch, Andrea   87

boa constrictors   xv, 25, 69, 70, 79

Bor, Paulus   88

Boyer, Anne   33

Bradshaw, Corey J. A.   99

Bríg   26

Bronx Zoo, New York   xv, 63, 70

Brook, Barry W.   73

Brooklyn Public Library,
New York   73
bull snakes   19
Bush, Barbara   28

caduceus   32
Center for Wildlife
Education, Georgia
Southern University,
Statesboro   3
Centers for Disease Control
and Prevention (CDC)
17
Cerrjón, Colombia   68
China   26
Clash of the Titans (Davis)
51
Claxton, Georgia, Chamber
of Commerce   2
Clifford, Mike   3–4
Clifton, Lucille   16
climate change   99, 107
cobras   6, 61, 63, 100
Cocullo, Italy   5–6
Collier, John   88
Collins, Britt   37
Columbian Exposition,
Chicago (1893)   23
Complex Rheology and
Biomechanics (CRAB)
Lab, Georgia Tech,
Atlanta   100, 101

Copenhagen, Denmark
xv
copperheads   xii, 13,
15, 43
coral snakes   37
cottonmouths   xii, 2, 10

Damajanti, Nala   24
Darwin, Charles   32
Davis, Mike   106
DeAndrade, Filipe   77
*Death of Truth, The:
Notes on Falsehood
in the Age of Trump*
(Kakutani)   92
defensive mimicry   77–8
Delacroix, Eugène   31, 89
Department of
Wildlife Ecology
& Conservation,
University of Florida,
Gainesville   10
Diaz, Natalie   78
Dickinson, Emily   72
Domenichino   88, 89

Eisenhower, Mamie   28
Eliot, T. S.   92
Elohim Creating Adam
(Blake)   89
Encyclopedia Britannica
68

Endangered Species International   61, 98
Essex Serpent, The (Perry) 69
Everglades National Park 55, 81

Facebook   12, 44, 63, 83
fashion and sexualization 21–30
Featherdale Wildlife Park, Australia   63
Festa dei Serpari, Cocullo, Italy   5
Florida   55–7
Florida Museum of Natural History, Gainesville 67, 74
Fortin, Boyd   1
Four Allegories: Falsehood (Wisdom) (Bellini) 87
Franklin, Benjamin   109
Fuss, Adam   86–7, 92

Gadsden Flag   xiiv, 24, 92
Gandhi, Lakshmi   34
garter snakes   xv, 6, 90
Georgia Department of Natural Resources   2
Giovanni Bellini (Goffen)   87

Goffen, Rona   88
Goldman, Daniel   100, 101, 102
Guardian   35, 37
Gugliotta, Guy   68

Haast, Bill   36, 38
Hanna, Jack   80
Harrison, Caroline Scott 28
Hein, Steven   3
herpetology   xiii, 3–4, 36, 73–4, 102, 105, 112
Hirshfield, Jane   77–8
Holy Ghost People (Adair)   42, 47, 48
Hoover, Lou Henny   28
How Snakes Work (Lillywhite)   99
Humane Rescue Alliance 59, 62, 64
Hurston, Zora Neale   91

"I'm a Slave 4 U" (Spears) 21
India   22, 23
indigos   3, 5, 15, 99
Instagram   63
invasive species   56–7, 81
Irwin, Robert   79, 80
Irwin, Steve   79, 80
Ivey, Bill   82

Jamestown, Virginia   55
Jennewein, C. Paul   73
Johnson, Lady Bird   28
Jörmungandr   26

Kakutani, Michiko   92
Keats, John   60, 78, 82, 94
Kennedy, Jacqueline   28
Kering   54
kingsnakes   3, 5, 62, 99
Kinski, Nastassja   25
Kwon, R. O.   84

La Charmeuse de serpents
    (Rousseau)   24
Lake Hopatcong, New
    Jersey   69, 70
Lamesa, Texas   9, 12,
    14, 18
"Lamia" (Keats)   94
Laocoön   xiii, 92
Laocoön and His Sons
    92–3
Las Vegas Natural History
    Museum   67
Lawrence, D. H.   91
Lemyre, Clara   105
Lilith (Collier)   88
Lillywhite, Harvey B.   99
Limón, Ada   78
Linton, Kristen   2, 6
Little Shop of Horrors
    (Oz)   69

Los Angeles Times   28
Ludwin, Steve   33,
    35–8, 43

Madagascar   25
Man and Snake, Vice TV
    34, 43
Mayan cultures   25
Medusa   51–3, 86, 87
Medusa (Fuss)   86
"Medusa" (Smith)   53
Metamorphoses (Ovid)
    52
Mexican Flag   xiv
Miami Serpentarium   36
*Midsummer Night's
    Dream, A*
    (Shakespeare)   24
Milton, John   14–16
Minoan Snake Goddess
    26
Miraculum (Post)   23
Mississippi Museum of
    Natural Science,
    Jackson   67–8
Mobile Matrix (Orozco)
    70, 72
monsters   70
    see also Titanoboa
    (*Titanoboa
    cerrejonensis*)
Moore, Booth   28
Morrison, Sarah R.   15, 16

mud snakes 73

Musée des Beaux-Arts, Paris 88

Museum of Modern Art (MoMA) 70

Musial, Jeff 80

mussuranas 99

Nag Panchami 6

Narcisse, Manitoba, Canada 6

National Geographic Wilds Untamed series 77

National Park Service 55

Native American cave drawings 93

Natural History Museum, London 35

negative capability 78, 82, 94

Netflix 67

New England Aquarium, Boston xv

New Orleans, Louisiana 59

New York Times 36

North Carolina 41

Obama, Michelle 28

Oklahoma 13

Oliver, Mary 60, 61

One More Generation 2

ophidiophobia xii, xiii, xiv, xv, 3, 4, 7, 9–10, 12, 15, 24, 30, 37, 62, 68–9, 79, 80, 83, 92, 98

Orianne Society 3

Orozco, Gabriel 70, 72

Outside 36

"Overprotected (Darkchild Remix)" (Spears) 26

Ovid 52

Paciorka, Brianna 105

Paradise Lost (Milton) 14–16

Pentecostal churches xv, 34, 35, 41, 43, 47

People Magazine 69

Perry, Sarah 69

Phantom Bodies: The Human Aura in Art, exhibition, Frist Art Museum, Nashville 86

Post, Steph 23

Proust Questionnaire 7

Python Conservation Partnership 54

pythons xv, 21, 24, 26, 30, 54–7, 59, 61, 80, 108, 109

Quetzalcoatl 26

Racy, A. J. 25–6
Raiders of the Lost Ark
(Spielberg) 7
Rainbow Serpent 26
rat snakes xii, 4, 6, 10, 90
Rattlesnake and Wildlife
Festival, Claxton,
Georgia xiii, 2–3, 7
Rattlesnake Roundup,
Sweetwater, Texas
1–2, 34
rattlesnakes xii, 1–3, 5, 7,
912, 17–19, 35, 43, 78,
91–2, 100, 109
Reagan, Nancy 28
*Rebuilding an Enlightened
World: Folklorizing
America* (Ivey) 82
*Rebuke of Adam
and Eve, The*
(Domenichino) 88,
89
Register Herald, West
Virginia 44
Reptile Magazine 70
Reptiles Alive LLC 79
Richards, Debbie and
Milton 9–15, 18–19
Rieser, Jennifer 101–2
ringnecks 63
Roosevelt, Eleanor 28
Roosevelt, Franklin D.
85, 86

roundups xiii, xiv, 1–2,
5, 7, 34
Rousseau, Henri 24
Ruane, Sarah 73–4

Salazar the Snake 60, 64
Satyanarayan, Kartrick
23
scarlet fever 32
Schiebel, Perrin 103, 104
Scrabble Creek, West
Virginia 42–9
Seitz, Caroline 79, 81
Serpents
anecdotes, mythology,
and superstitions
xiii, xiv–xv, 4–6, 11,
23–6, 37, 51–3, 60, 69,
73, 86, 87, 106
in arts and popular
culture xii, xiii, 4, 7,
14–17, 21–2, 23–8, 31,
33–5, 68–9, 73, 77–81,
86, 87–94
in ceremonies and
festivals 4–5, 6
characteristics xv, 3
conservation and
education xv, 2–4,
23, 87–99, 105–6, 107
deaths from 14, 23, 109
and ecosystems 10,
38–9, 55–7, 81, 99

euphemisms 63, 65, 98
in fashion 51, 53–4, 56–7
in medicine and research xiii, 6, 33, 34, 35, 37, 100–4
as pets 61, 63, 66, 70
in religion xv, 5, 11, 15–17, 34, 41–50, 59, 80–1, 89
as symbols xiii–xiv, 5, 16, 25, 33–5, 37, 58, 92, 109
wildlife education 79–80, 83
Seshamani, Geeta 22
Shakespeare, William 24, 78
Shiva 26
Shovel-noses 101–3
sidewinders *see* rattlesnakes
signs following xv, 35–50
sleep paralysis 85–6
Smith, Patricia 53
Smithsonian Institution, Washington, DC
National Museum of American History 28
National Museum of Natural History 94
Smithsonian Magazine 67, 68

snakebites 5, 11, 14, 17–18, 23, 36, 37, 41, 88, 92, 97, 109
snake charming 21–3
snake handling 41–50
snake identification 12, 83–4
"Snake-Light" (Diaz) 78
"snake oil" cons 34–5
Snakes on a Plane (Ellis) xiii–xiv, 95
Sodhi, Navjot S. 99
"Some Questions You Might Ask" (Oliver) 61
Songs of Experience (Blake) 89
Songs of Innocence (Blake) 89
South Florida Water Management District 57
Spears, Britney xv, 21–2, 24, 26, 29–30
"Sweat" (Hurston) 89, 91

Temple of Pythons, Benin 59
Tennessee 10, 41
Tennessee Aquarium, Chattanooga xiii, 68
The Cut 84

"Thoreau's Hound: Poetry and the Hidden" (Hirshfield) 77–8

Tiger and Snake (Delacroix) 31, 89

Titanoboa (*Titanoboa cerrejonensis*) xiii, 67, 68, 71–3

Transcontinental Railroad 34

Twitter 63, 70

Undying, The (Boyer) 35

University of Copenhagen, Denmark 35

University of Notre Dame, Notre Dame 29

Vanity Fair 7

venom xii, xiii, 7–12, 14–16, 29, 31, 33, 73, 80, 87

Versace, Gianni 51, 53, 57–8

Video Music Awards 21

vipers 61, 90, 99

Virginia Herpetological Society 4

voodoo 59

Voodoo Museum, New Orleans, Louisiana 59

Wallace, Laney 2

Washington, Martha 28

water snakes 4, 34, 69, 90

West Virginia xv

White, Stanford 73

"Wild Geese" (Oliver) 60

Wildlife SOS 22

Williams, Iolo 97

Zoo Atlanta 100, 102

Zoo Knoxville 104–6

OBJECT LESSONS

Cross them all off your list.

exit

9781501358159

political sign

9781501358104

gin

9781501353277

bulletproof vest

9781501353024

coffee

9781501344350

environment

9781501361906

"Perfect for slipping in a pocket and pulling out when life is on hold."

– Toronto Star

9781501353352

9781501348815

9781501348518

9781501348631

9781501325991

9781501307409

Burger by Carol J. Adams

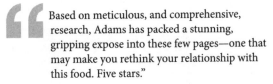

Based on meticulous, and comprehensive, research, Adams has packed a stunning, gripping expose into these few pages—one that may make you rethink your relationship with this food. Five stars."

San Francisco Book Review

Adams would seem the least likely person to write about hamburgers with her philosophically lurid antipathy to carnivory. But if the point is to deconstruct this iconic all-American meal, then she is the woman for the job."

Times Higher Education

It's tempting to say that *Burger* is a literary meal that fills the reader's need, but that's the essence of Adams' quick, concise, rich exploration of the role this meat (or meatless) patty has played in our lives."

PopMatters

High Heel by Summer Brennan

❝ a kaleidoscopic view of feminine public existence, both wide-ranging and thoughtful."

Jezebel

❝ Brennan makes the case that high heels are an apt metaphor for the ways in which women have been hobbled in their mobility. She also tackles the relationship between beauty and suffering, highlighting the fraught nature of reclaiming objects defined under patriarchy for feminism."

Paste Magazine

❝ From Cinderella's glass slippers to Carrie Bradshaw's Manolo Blahniks, Summer Brennan deftly analyzes one of the world's most provocative and sexualized fashion accessories . . . Whether you see high heels as empowering or a submission to patriarchal gender roles (or land somewhere in between), you'll likely never look at a pair the same way again after reading *High Heel*."

Longreads

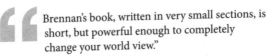

Brennan's book, written in very small sections, is short, but powerful enough to completely change your world view."

Refinery29

In *High Heel*, the wonderful Summer Brennan embraces a slippery, electric conundrum: Does the high heel stand for oppression or power? . . . *High Heel* elevates us, keeps us off balance, and sharpens the point."

The Philadelphia Inquirer

Hood by Alison Kinney

Provocative and highly informative, Alison Kinney's *Hood* considers this seemingly neutral garment accessory and reveals it to be vexed by a long history of violence, from the Grim Reaper to the KKK and beyond—a history we would do well to address, and redress. Readers will never see hoods the same way again."

Sister Helen Prejean, author of
Dead Man Walking

"*Hood* is searing. It describes the historical properties of the hood, but focuses on this object's modern-day connotations. Notably, it dissects the racial fear evoked by young black men in hoodies, as shown by the senseless killings of unarmed black males. It also touches on U.S. service members' use of hoods to mock and torture prisoners at Abu Ghraib. Hoods can represent the (sometimes toxic) power of secret affiliations, from monks to Ku Klux Klan members. And clearly they can also be used by those in power to dehumanize others. In short, *Hood* does an excellent job of unspooling the many faces of hoods."

Book Riot

[*Hood*] is part of a series entitled Object Lessons, which looks at 'the hidden lives of ordinary things' and which are all utterly 'Fridge Brilliant' (defined by TV Tropes as an experience of sudden revelation, like the light coming on when you open a refrigerator door). . . . In many ways *Hood* isn't about hoods at all. It's about what—and who—is under the hood. It's about the hooding, the hooders and the hoodees . . . [and] identity, power and politics. . . . Kinney's book certainly reveals the complex history of the hood in America."

London Review of Books

Personal Stereo by
Rebecca Tuhus-Dubrow

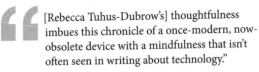

[Rebecca Tuhus-Dubrow's] thoughtfulness imbues this chronicle of a once-modern, now-obsolete device with a mindfulness that isn't often seen in writing about technology."

Pitchfork (named one of *Pitchfork's* favorite books of 2017)

After finishing *Personal Stereo*, I found myself wondering about the secret lives of every object around me, as if each device were whispering, 'Oh, I am much so more than meets the eye' . . . Tuhus-Dubrow is a master researcher and synthesizer. . . . *Personal Stereo* is a joy to read."

Los Angeles Review of Books

Personal Stereo is loving, wise, and exuberant, a moving meditation on nostalgia and obsolescence. Rebecca Tuhus-Dubrow writes as beautifully about Georg Simmel and Allan Bloom as she does about Jane Fonda and Metallica. Now I understand why I still own the taxicab-yellow Walkman my grandmother gave me in 1988."

Nathaniel Rich, author of *Odds Against Tomorrow*

[A] careful, astute study."

The Wire

Souvenir by Rolf Potts

" Rolf Potts writes with the soul of an explorer
and a scholar's love of research. Much like the
objects that we bestow with meaning, this book
carries a rich, lingering resonance. A gem."

Andrew McCarthy, actor, director, and author of
The Longest Way Home (2013)

" *Souvenir*, a sweet new book by Rolf Potts, is a
little gem (easily tucked into a jacket pocket)
filled with big insights . . . *Souvenir* explores our
passions for such possessions and why we are
compelled to transport items from one spot to
another."

Forbes

" A treasure trove of . . . fascinating deep dives into
the history of travel keepsakes . . . Potts walks us
through the origins of some of the most popular
vacation memorabilia, including postcards
and the still confoundedly ubiquitous souvenir
spoons. He also examines the history of the more
somber side of mementos, those depicting crimes
and tragedies. Overall, the book, as do souvenirs
themselves, speaks to the broader issues of time,
memory, adventure, and nostalgia."

The Boston Globe

Veil by Rafia Zakaria

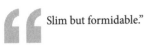

Slim but formidable."

London Review of Books

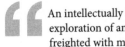

Rafia Zakaria's *Veil* shifts the balance away from white secular Europe toward the experience of Muslim women, mapping the stereotypical representations of the veil in Western culture and then reflecting, in an intensely personal way, on the many meanings that the veil can have for the people who wear it . . . [*Veil* is] useful and important, providing needed insight and detail to deepen our understanding of how we got here—a necessary step for thinking about whether and how we might be able to move to a better place."

The Nation

An intellectually bracing, beautifully written exploration of an item of clothing all too freighted with meaning."

Molly Crabapple, artist, journalist, and author of *Drawing Blood* (2015)